From Bad Credit to Your Financial Freedom

The Complete Guide to Credit Repair and Money Management

Eesa Kaysir

Copyrighted Material

From Bad Credit to Your Financial Freedom: The Complete Guide to Credit Repair and Money Management © 2024 Eesa Kaysir

No part of this publication may be reproduced, distributed, or transmitted in any form or by any means, including photocopying, recording, or other electronic or mechanical methods, without the publisher's prior written permission, with the exception of brief quotations in critical reviews and certain other noncommercial uses permitted by copyright law. For permission requests, contact the author at

kindle.eesa@gmail.com.

Published by Amazon Kindle Direct

Publishing (KDP). This book is a work of non-fiction. The advice and strategies contained herein may not be suitable for every situation. This work is sold with the understanding that the publisher and the author are not engaged in rendering legal, accounting, or other professional services. If professional assistance is required, the services of a competent professional should be sought.

Copyright © 2024 Eesa Kaysir

All rights reserved

ISBN: 9798329557435

Copyrighted Material

DEDICATION

To my parents, whose unwavering support and encouragement have been my guiding light.

To my mentors and friends, who have always believed in me and offered their wisdom.

To everyone striving to achieve financial freedom, this book is for you. May it guide you on your journey toward a secure and prosperous future.

And to my readers, for whom I have written this book, with the hope that it will be a valuable resource in your quest for financial empowerment and stability. May you find the knowledge and inspiration within these pages to transform your financial life.

Table of Contents

Chapter 01: Understanding The Banking System 7
- Understanding Our Banking System 7
- Procedure to Write A Check, Withdraw Money, Deposit Money 11
- Understanding a Credit Card 18
- Credit Cards vs. Debit Cards 20
- Benefits of Using a Credit Card 22
- How to Choose Your First Credit Card 25
- Important Credit Card Terms 26

Chapter 02: Credit Report & Credit Scores 28
- Credit Reports 28
- Credit Scores 29
- FICO Score – Popular Credit Scoring Model 31
- What Can Hurt Your Credit Score 34
- Negative Items on Your Credit Report 36

Chapter 03: Credit Repairing 39
- Introduction to Credit Repair 39
- The DIY Method for Credit Repair 40
- What Can You Do to Improve a Bad Credit 42
- Credit Repair Service Companies 43
- Ways to Evaluate Credit Repair Companies 44
- Quick Tips for Repairing Your Credit 45

Chapter 04: Credit Boosting 48
- How to Increase Your Credit Score by Removing Negative Items ... 48
- The Most Effective Ways to Boost Your Credit Score 49

Why Your Credit History Is Important 53

The reasons why credit history holds crucial importance are being stated below.. 53

How to Establish a Credit History and Establish Creditworthiness ... 54

How to Maintain Your Credit Health Over Time 55

Chapter 05: Money Management Tactics 57

Introduction to Money Management... 57

Money Management Principles... 57

The Critical Importance of Saving 60

Tips for Saving Money.. 63

How to Spend Money Wisely 65

Ways to Make a Plan to Spend Money 66

Understanding Budgeting and Its Importance..................................... 68

Different Budgeting Strategies.. 71

Emergency Funds.. 74

Sinking Funds 75

First Thing You Should Do with Every Paycheck.............................. 76

Automate Your Finances... 78

Useful tools for Managing your Finances 79

Chapter 06: Paying Off Student Loans 83

How Budgeting After College Can Help Repay Student Loans 83

Ways to Make A Plan To Pay Off Student Loans............................... 84

How To Avoid Defaulting On Student Loans..................................... 86

Tips For Managing Your Student Loan Debt...................................... 87

Chapter 07: Investing for Increasing Your Assets 90

Understanding Investing 90

Learning How the Stock Market Works 93

Functions of a Stock Market 97

Individual Retirement Account (IRA) vs Non-Retirement Brokerage Accounts.. 99

Index Fund 102

Target-Date vs. Index Funds 104

Dollar Cost Averaging vs. Lump Sum Investing 106

How to invest: step-by-step... 111

Layers of Investing... 114

Chapter 01: Understanding The Banking System

Understanding Our Banking System

Banks are a crucial aspect of our lives. We deposit checks, borrow money, and save at banks. So what do banks do? What types of banks exist? Examine the numerous types of banks in a financial system to find solutions.

Banking systems are networks of financial service providers. These companies handle payments, loans, deposits, and investments.

Functions of the Banking System

1. Banks, both physical and online, facilitate the flow of money between individuals and businesses.
2. They provide deposit accounts as secure places for people to store their money.
3. Banks lend money to individuals and businesses using funds from deposit accounts.
4. Borrowers pay interest on loans, and part of that interest is returned to the deposit account holder, typically for savings, money market, or CD accounts.
5. Banks generate revenue from loan interest and fees paid by customers.
6. Costs may be associated with specific services or financial products, such as bank accounts or investment services.
7. Investment banks offering portfolio management may charge fees for their services.
8. Banking is closely regulated, with the Federal Reserve System overseeing banks and collaborating with state regulatory bodies to ensure compliance.

9. Other government entities like the Federal Deposit Insurance Corporation (FDIC), the Office of Thrift Supervision (OTS), and the Office of the Comptroller of the Currency (OCC) monitor banks to maintain standards.

Types of Banks

The word "bank" can refer to a number of different types of financial institutions. Different types of banks offer different goods and services and have different jobs to do. It's important to know the differences between them. Some of them are consumer-facing, which means they work directly with regular people. Others are more involved in the big picture of how money moves in the economy. Look under the awning over the bank. The following will be found:

Here is more information about what each type of bank is supposed to do and how it works.

Central Banks

Central banks are in charge of a country's or a group of countries' money. These groups are in charge of making monetary policy, keeping an eye on how currencies change, and setting interest rate benchmarks. To put it simply, they are what hold a country's financial system together.

Among other places, the Federal Reserve is the central bank in the United States. There are twelve regional federal banks that make up the Federal Reserve System. When the Federal Reserve holds securities, it earns money by paying interest on those securities. The bank sends its net income to the US Treasury.

In the Federal Reserve System, banks are in charge of four different tasks, which are:

- keeping an eye on and inspecting state member banks
- Giving loans to banks and other depositories

- Giving the government important financial services to help run the country's payment system

- Looking at financial institutions

In the United States, these services are essential to banking. They let you do everything from applying for a mortgage to using your debit card to buy things online.

Retail Banks

When most people think of banks, they think of small, local banks. People and small businesses can use these banks' loans, savings accounts, and other financial services. Retail banks can be real places with branches or online banks where you can only use an app to handle your money.

Not-for-profit groups that offer banking services might also be in this group. As an example, more and more fintech companies, called neobanks, offer deposit accounts that are like those at banks. Even though they are not banks themselves, these companies work with other banks to offer FDIC-insured banking products and services.

Commercial Banks

Commercial banks mostly take care of the needs of businesses and corporations, but they can also help people who just want to use their services.

Consumer banks and commercial banks are both able to lend money, accept deposits, and offer other banking services like international banking and payment processing.

In general, commercial banks do a lot of different things. For instance, a commercial bank might lend money for things like real estate or business equipment, but it would charge interest and fees for the privilege of lending money. The same financial institution can offer both business and personal banking services.

Investment Banks

Trading securities, managing investor accounts, or a mix of the two are all things that investment banks can do. You can use an investment bank as a go-between for investors who want to get into the markets by helping you buy or sell securities. They can also give customers advice on how to invest their money.

In addition to helping regular investors, investment banks do other things as well. For instance, when a company is thinking about going public for the first time, they help with the underwriting process (IPO). An investment bank may also help businesses merge or buy other businesses.

Shadow Banks

Shadow banks are not the same as regular banks in terms of what they do and how they are regulated. These financial companies that aren't banks aren't regulated very much, and they mostly buy credit and debt securities. Insurance companies and hedge funds are examples of shadow banking organizations.

Credit Unions

A lot of the same things are done by credit unions, which are also called cooperative financial institutions. The main difference is that credit unions are not for profit like regular banks. Credit unions are run by "members," who pool their money and set the rules for the business. You have to be a member of a credit union to open an account. Some of these criteria could be based on where someone lives, their job, their religious beliefs, or their time in the military. Not the FDIC, but the National Credit Union Administration often backs up credit unions (NCUA).

Procedure to Write A Check, Withdraw Money, Deposit Money

Procedure to write a check

People who write checks often will find the process almost automatic. But this might be hard to understand if you haven't written many checks before. Electronic transfers are taking the place of checks, but checks are still valid. These steps will show you how to fill out a check and explain the numbers that are already on each one.

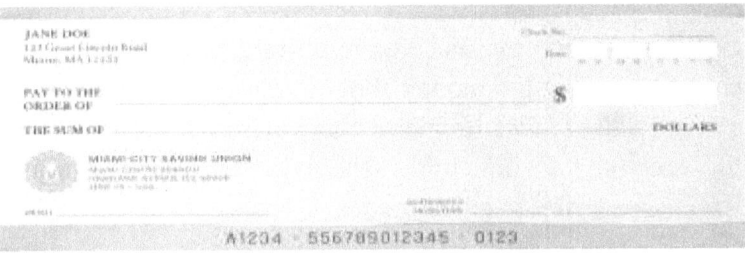

Source: https://www.freepik.com/

- **Date.** On the check's blank line in the upper right corner, write the date. It tells the bank when you wrote the check and if it is postdated, which means it should be cashed on or after the date written on the check.

- **Recipient's name.** In the space after "Pay to the Order Of," write the name of the person you mean to pay. No matter who gets the check, this could be a person, an organization, or a business. When talking about a person, use both the first and last name. When talking about a business or organization, use the full name.

- **Amount (numerical form).** Kindly enter the dollar amount in the space to the right of the recipient's name. Instead of writing a new amount, write the amount as close to the left side of the check as you can.

- **Amount (expanded word form).** Kindly enter the dollar amount in the space to the right of the recipient's name. Instead of writing a new amount, write the amount as close to the left side of the check as you can.

- **Signature.** Sign your name on the line in the bottom right corner of the check. The person who receives the check needs your signature to be able to cash it. If you signed the check but forgot to hand it over or mail it, make sure you did it twice.

- **Memo (optional).** A line is at the bottom left where you can write down or type in the account number for the company, like the utility company, that you're writing the check for. Plus, it could mean that the money should be used to pay off what you owe instead of something else. Say you're writing a check to pay for something at your child's school. In the memo line, you could write his or her name and grade.

Procedure to Withdraw Money from Your Bank Account

You might be wondering how you can get to the money in your bank account so that you can spend it, pay your bills, or maybe even repay your best friend. So you can rest easy knowing that you have a lot of easy options to choose from.

Use an ATM

If you have an ATM card or a debit card linked to your bank account, you can get cash from an ATM. There are some small differences between ATMs, but in general, you just put in your debit card, enter your PIN, choose which account you want to take money out of (if you have more than one), enter the amount you want to take out and wait for the ATM to give you cash and a receipt.

To keep things simple, many ATMs only let you take out twenty dollars at a time. There may also be limits on how much cash you can take out at once or in a single day. Also, many banks let you take out cash from their ATMs for free, but if you go to an ATM that isn't part of your bank's network, you might have to pay a fee (i.e., it is operated by a different bank or financial organization).

Lastly, make sure you get your ATM card before you walk or drive away. If you don't, you could lose it or have fraud happen on your account.

Write a Check for Cash

If you have a checking account, money market account, or any other type of account that lets you write checks, you can write "cash" in the write-to line of a check. Then, take your check to the bank teller along with your ID. This person will give you cash if they have enough money in their account. Be careful when you type "cash." People who find the lost or stolen check may be able to cash it right away, which means you could lose your money.

Fill Out a Withdrawal Slip

At the branch near you, you can fill out a withdrawal slip if your account doesn't have checks linked to it. Don't forget to write down the date, the account name, and the account number. One of the tellers can look up your account number if you don't have it. They can use your ID and/or debit card. Then, type in how much money you want to get. Talk to your teller or banker if you have any questions.

Connect Your Account with a Peer-to-Peer Payment Service

The way we trade money with each other is also becoming more and more digital. You can get to your money in another way by connecting your account to a third-party peer-to-peer (P2P) payment provider, like Venmo or PayPal. These are more and more common ways to thank a friend for getting you a cappuccino or for the ridesharing service you used last weekend. To keep your account safe and secure, use PINs, set your account to private, and turn on alerts to stay on top of account activity. Also, make sure that only people you know and trust use these services. Getting good at withdrawing will take some time.

Procedure to deposit money into your bank account

Make a deposit at a bank or credit union branch.

In-person deposits at banks and credit unions are the easiest way to fund your account. The type, quantity, and dollar amount of payments you can deposit are also the most flexible with it. A deposit slip is usually required to deposit money at a bank. Each bank's deposit slip includes its name and perhaps routing number. You can use the preprinted deposit slips your bank or credit union gave you when you opened your account or a lobby-available blank slip. Filling it out correctly ensures timely and accurate deposit of funds.

Fill Out A Deposit Slip

Source: https://www.freepik.com/

- ☑ **Your name:** On this line, write your first name, middle initial, and last name.
- ☑ **Your address:** Fill in the blanks with your street address, city, state, and ZIP code.
- ☑ **Your account number:** Your checkbook or savings account statements usually have the account number in the middle. Log in to your online account to access it.
- ☑ **Date of the deposit:** Make a note of the date you're making the deposit.
- ☑ **Amount of the deposit:** The right side of the deposit sheet usually has several lines with single-space boxes for one number. List the total amount of cash you're depositing in the specified area, then list each check with its number and amount in the box.
- ☑ **Cash back:** On the line for check deposits from which you're taking cash, write down how much cash you want back.
- ☑ **Total deposit:** Add up all the deposits and write the result in the subtotal box. Take away any cash-back amounts and enter the amount of money that's left in the "total" field.

Keep in mind that checks must usually be endorsed before they may be deposited.

Deposit Money at An ATM

There is no need to use an ATM that is connected to your bank's network to deposit cash or a check. You can do it at any ATM that also takes deposits. It will take longer if you are not using your own bank's equipment.

Before you go to the ATM, you should count your money and sign your checks. To make a deposit, put in your debit or ATM card and follow the on-screen instructions. The most likely things you'll need to do to make an ATM deposit are these:

- ☑ Put your debit card in and enter your PIN to get into your account. You could also use a mobile wallet to make an ATM transaction without touching the machine.
- ☑ Pick "deposit" from the list of transaction types.
- ☑ Pick out the account where you want the money to go.
- ☑ If you are given an envelope, put your cash inside it and write down any information that is asked for on it. Put the cash and/or checks into the machine when asked.
- ☑ Please wait for your money. Keep it somewhere safe in case something goes wrong with your deposit.

Mobile Check Deposit

When you deposit a check from your phone, you don't need to fill out a deposit slip. You can only get to your bank account online through a mobile banking app on your phone at most banks.

Here are the steps that need to be taken:

1. Log in to your account.
2. Snap a photo of your check.
3. A confirmation of the desired monetary amount and other information is asked.
4. Your mobile deposit is made.

More options for depositing funds into your bank account

You can make deposits in more ways than just the usual ways, like in-branch, ATM, and smartphone deposits. Take a look at these other examples:

- **Direct deposit:** Direct deposit lets you get things like paychecks and government benefits sent straight to your bank account. You can sign up online to get help from the government. For direct deposit of your paychecks, fill out a form given to you by your bank or employer.

- **Account transfer:** If you have more than one bank account, you can use mobile or internet banking to move money from one account to another and then deposit it.

- **External transfer:** You can join accounts from different banks with some financial institutions.

  Once you have linked two accounts, you can move money between them by following the bank's instructions, which you can usually find in online banking.

- **Wire transfer:** A wire transfer is what someone does to send you money from a different bank account or through a service like Western Union or MoneyGram. You and they may both be charged a fee, but wire transfers are safe and can usually be done right away. If someone sends you money, they will need to see your bank information. Don't accept a transfer from a business or someone you don't know well.

- **Peer-to-peer transfer:** You can receive money from other people using apps and platforms for sending money, like Zelle, Venmo, and PayPal. You can transfer the money to your linked bank account if the app doesn't send the payment right away. Please keep in mind that the amount of a transaction may be limited, and you may have to pay a fee.

Understanding a Credit Card

A credit card is a thin, oval piece of hard plastic that you can get from a bank or other financial service company. It lets you borrow money to pay for things at stores that accept cards. Credit cards have rules that say cardholders have to pay back the money they borrowed plus interest and any other conditional charges, either in full by the due date or over time. In this case, the Chase Sapphire Reserve is a credit card. You can read our honest review of the Chase Sapphire Reserve credit card to get a good idea of what the card is really like.

Different types of Credit Cards
Cashback Credit Cards

With a cashback credit card, it's easy to get cash back or statement credits for the things you buy. However, each card has its own rules about how rewards are given out. There are options in this slot that pay out a flat rate of dividends and options that give bonus points for things like traveling. Some even offer flat reward rates on all purchases, without bonus rates, as well as bonus rates in categories that change every three months

Rewards Credit Cards

There are different kinds of rewards credit cards, and some of them even give you cash back. Most rewards credit cards give you points based on a percentage of what you spend. Some even give you extra points for things like groceries, gas, dining out, and a lot of other common categories.

Travel Credit Cards

With a travel credit card, you can earn rewards that are designed to help you travel. For example, you could earn flexible travel credits that you can use on any trip or points that you can transfer to airline or hotel programs. You can earn points in certain programs with some travel credit cards. These programs could be frequent flyers or hotel loyalty programs.

Balance Transfer Credit Cards

People who have a lot of high-interest credit card debt might think about using a balance transfer credit card to help them manage and pay off their debt. The simplest balance transfer cards offer a 0% introductory APR for a period of time, usually between 15 and 21 months. This may be a nice break from paying interest while you focus on paying off your loans. Some credit cards don't charge a fee to transfer a balance, but most do. The fee is usually between 3% and 5% of the amount you want to transfer. With the introductory APR offer on your card, you'll save a lot of money on interest, even when you take into account the balance transfer fee.

Low-Interest Credit Cards

There are also many credit cards that offer purchases with no interest for a certain amount of time, usually up to 18 months. If you want to make an investment outside of your own country and need to pay it back over time without interest, this kind of credit card is often a blessing. In the same way, there are credit cards with low-interest rates that have rates that are lower than average all the time, not just during an introductory offer phase.

Business Credit Cards

People who have business credit cards can keep their personal and business costs separate and earn rewards on all of their business spending. A strange thing about business credit cards is that they can also be cash-back cards, general rewards cards, travel credit cards, or even secured credit cards. To get a business credit card, you need to have a business or do something that makes money.

Student Credit Cards

Student credit cards are like "starter credit cards" because they are made for kids who don't have much credit history. That is, the requirements for applications aren't as strict, which makes it easier to get approval. You won't have to pay an annual fee for most student credit cards, and many of them give you extra benefits every time you use them, like rewards for every dollar you spend. Getting a student credit card can help kids build credit and learn good money habits as long as they use it wisely.

Secured Credit Cards

Most credit cards are "unsecured," which means you don't have to put anything up as security. Secured credit cards, on the other hand, require you to put down a small amount of cash to protect a small line of credit, usually for the same amount. On the other hand, you might apply for a secured credit card and put down a $500 deposit to get a $500 line of credit. Most of the time, the credit limit and one-time deposit are both as low as $49.

Store Credit Cards

When people use this kind of card in stores, they can charge their purchases and pay for them over time. Most of the time, store credit cards can only be used in the store that issued them. However, some store credit cards can be used in a certain group of stores.

Co-Branded Credit Cards

Co-branded credit cards are credit cards with the brand of a regular credit card company, like American Express, Citi, Chase, or Citibank. Some examples are credit cards from airlines that let you earn miles in a certain frequent flyer program and credit cards from hotels that let you earn points in a hotel loyalty program. Some co-branded credit cards work with stores, but you'll probably use them to buy things online instead.

Credit Cards vs. Debit Cards

A lot of people get credit cards and debit cards mixed up because they look so much alike. We'll look at what they have in common and what makes them different to help you tell them apart.

Similarities

Cards that let you get money out of an account are known as debit or credit cards. You can use any kind of card to buy anything you want. The ways you can do business with them financially are also the same. The most common way to buy something in person is to insert or swipe a card into a reader. When you buy something online, you have to enter your credit card information by hand.

Differences

Feature	Credit Card	Debit Card
Linked Account Type	Line of Credit	Bank Account
Transaction Process	The card issuer makes the first payment; the cardholder pays later	Money is directly deducted from the bank account
Usage for Payments	It can be used repeatedly with a credit limit	Uses the available funds in the linked bank account
Disputing Unauthorized Charges	Call the number on the back of the card; the issuer investigates	Report to the bank, which investigates before refunding money
Fraud Protection Process	The card issuer addresses fake charges, providing a refund	Bank investigates debit card fraud before reimbursing victim
Safety Perception	It may be perceived as a safer payment method	Considered less secure due to potential delays in resolution

Credit score

When you use a debit card, it doesn't hurt your credit score like a credit card does. To raise your credit score, all you have to do is use credit cards wisely and make payments on time. It won't help your credit score to use a debit card to buy something.

Secured credit cards

These credit cards need a collateral deposit to be approved. They are called "secured credit cards." People with bad or limited credit often choose them over regular credit cards that don't require collateral.

To get a secured credit card, you have to put down a deposit. However, these cards are still credit cards and not debit cards. You still owe money on your credit cards. There is only the deposit to protect you. One more thing is that using a secured card responsibly may help you build credit, just like using any other credit card.

Benefits of Using a Credit Card

You walk into a department store, choose a pair of running shoes, and then go to the register to pay. You pull out your credit card, pay, and then leave the store. The process was very easy and only took a few minutes. No one will question how sure your bank is that you can pay back the shoes it gave you on credit.

You don't have to go to a bank, fill out any forms, or explain why you need the money. Instead, you could use a credit card to buy anything, only pay interest on the amount you carry, and settle the balance whenever it works best for you. The retail industry has changed a lot because credit cards make it easy and quick to get large amounts of credit. These days, it's common to pay for things with plastic, and you might have credit cards from more than one bank.

The vast majority of banks and other financial institutions offer different types of credit cards. They may be used to being able to buy clothes, groceries, and services anywhere that takes them. Credit cards can be used to buy many things, like groceries, clothes and accessories, movie tickets, things to do online, home appliances, utility bills, and cell phone bills.

There are many good things about credit cards, but here are some of the most important ones:

1. Buy on credit

One of the best things about a credit card is how much credit it can give you. If your balance is less than or equal to that amount, you can buy anything you want without having to pay for it right away. It won't have a big effect on your monthly budget if you buy expensive things on credit. One great thing about using a credit card is that you can break up the cost of your purchases into easy-to-repay installments. The result of this has been nothing less than revolutionary for stores.

2. Most accepted method of payment

With this card, you don't need to carry around a lot of cash. You can go anywhere in the world. The most convenient way to pay is with a credit card, which can be used almost anywhere.

3. Interest-free cash withdrawals

Some credit cards let you take out an emergency withdrawal up to a certain amount, and for the first 45 or 50 days, you don't have to pay interest. The money can be used for any important financial needs that come up quickly.

4. Unlimited reward points

You can earn reward points every time you use one of these cards. For example, IDFC FIRST Bank credit cards come with reward points that can be redeemed for cash at any time.

5. Insurance coverage

A lot of people like credit cards because they come with perks like personal accident and travel insurance.

6. Make travel easy

On the road, credit cards are very useful because you can use them in so many places. If you have an IDFC FIRST Bank credit card, you can get extra benefits like faster check-in and free use of lounges at Indian airports and train stations. There are also deals at more than 280 different restaurants.

7. Discounts and cashback

You can save money at popular restaurants, travel sites, shopping apps, and more when you use a credit card. As a bonus, all gas stations across the country will get rid of the extra fees that are usually added to buying gas.

8. Improve your credit score

Not only can credit cards help you buy things on credit, but they may also help your credit score. To improve your CIBIL score, use your credit card wisely by doing things like paying off all of your purchases on time and in full. That will make it much easier for you to apply for loans in the future.

9. Offers safety

Credit cards have made it so that you don't have to carry around huge amounts of cash.

10. Keep track of your expenses

Your online bank will send you a statement every month that will help you keep track of your spending and plan ahead for payments.

How to Choose Your First Credit Card

A lot of the features and benefits that come with beginner credit cards are made with people who have never had a credit card before in mind. These things should be in a good first credit card.

No annual fee

It's best to keep your first credit card open for as long as you want since that will add months to your credit history. If you want to save money every year, start with a credit card that doesn't charge an annual fee.

Free FICO® Score tracker

With some credit cards, you can get your FICO® Score for free. This way, you can check your credit score right from your credit card account.

No or low-security deposit

When people get their first credit card, they often choose a secured card. To get this type of card, you have to pay a security deposit that you can get back. When applicants have to pay a deposit before getting the card, the credit card company is more likely to give them one.

You shouldn't just think about secured credit cards; you should also think about unsecured ones. This could mean that you don't have to put down a security deposit. If you decide to go that route, look for a secured card with a low deposit amount. It's a good deal to get a credit card that only needs a $200 deposit in exchange for $100 in credit.

Rewards

It's not very important that you earn points on a starter card because its main purpose is to help you build credit so that you can get better rates on loans and cards in the future. Even so, if your first credit card has rewards, that's not a bad thing to have.

Important Credit Card Terms

Credit card: A physical card used to access a financial account online. You may use the card to make purchases using the associated credit line.

Unsecured credit card: No-guarantee credit cards allow cardholders to make purchases without first providing a security deposit. Unsecured credit cards are the norm.

Secured credit card: A kind of credit card that calls for an initial deposit from the cardholder.

Cash advance: Making a cash withdrawal using a credit card. It is not advisable to get a cash advance because of the high interest rates and the fact that interest is charged from the moment the money is borrowed.

Balance transfer: Balancing your accounts by moving your debt from one credit card to another, often to take advantage of a cheaper interest rate. This benefit is not available on all credit cards.

Credit limit: The highest possible balance on a credit card. Credit cards' withdrawal limitations for cash advances might vary widely. For instance, a card could allow you to withdraw $3,000 from a cash advance but just $10,000 in total. A maximum cash advance of $3,000 is permitted under the $10,000 credit limit.

Available credit: Distinction between a cardholder's total credit potential and their actual credit use. If your credit card has a $1,000 limit and you've spent $400, you'll have $600 left.

Revolving line of credit: A kind of credit from which you may take out loans up to a certain amount so long as the account is in good standing.

APR: The yearly interest rate, or APR, is the rate at which borrowing money costs you.

Minimum payment: The least amount that may be charged to your credit card and yet have it be paid in whole by the due date. A late fee may be assessed by the card issuer if you don't pay at least this amount by the due date.

Statement balance: The amount due on your credit card as of the last day of your most recent billing cycle. You may prevent paying interest on purchases by making this payment in full every billing cycle.

Credit score: A credit score is a number that indicates how likely it is that you will pay back the money you borrow.

Chapter 02: Credit Report & Credit Scores

Credit Reports

A credit report is a piece of paper that shows your current credit standing and your financial history. It includes information about your loan balances and how well you're paying back your loans. A lot of people have more than one credit report. Credit reporting companies, which are also called credit bureaus or consumer reporting agencies, keep track of the financial information that lenders, credit card companies, and other financial institutions send them about you. Creditors don't have to report to all credit bureaus.

That's how lenders decide if they want to lend you money and how much interest to charge you. Also, lenders will check your credit report to see if you are still meeting the terms of a credit account you already have. There are other businesses that might look at your credit report to decide if they want to insure you, rent you a house or apartment, or give you cable TV, internet, utility, or cell phone service. If you give an employer permission to look at your credit report, they may use it to decide whether to hire you.

The following information is often found on credit reports:

Personal information

- Your name and any aliases you may have used in the past in connection with a credit account
- Current and former addresses
- Birth date
- Social Security number
- Phone numbers

Credit Accounts

- Current and previous credit accounts, including account type (mortgage, installment, revolving, etc.)
- The credit limit or amount
- Account balance
- Account payment history
- The date the account was opened and closed
- The name of the creditor

Credit Scores

A number between 300 and 850 shows how creditworthy someone is. Lenders are more likely to lend money to someone whose score is higher. One's credit score is based on their credit history, which includes things like the number of open accounts, total debt, and payment history. Lenders use credit scores to figure out how likely it is that a borrower will pay back loans on time.

These are the only three credit bureaus in the US that have national power: Equifax, Experian, and TransUnion. This trio is the best at gathering, analyzing, and sharing data about people who use the credit market. The credit score model was made by the Fair Isaac Corp., which is now called FICO. It is used by banks and other financial institutions. There are other ways to score credit, but the FICO Score is by far the most popular.

People can raise their credit scores by paying off their debts on time and not taking on too much debt.

How Credit Scores Work

Your credit score could have a big effect on how much money you have. It plays a big role in a lender's choice of whether to give you credit. Subprime borrowers are people whose credit scores are less than 640, for example. Lenders usually charge higher interest rates on subprime mortgages than on regular mortgages to make up for the extra risk they are taking. People with bad credit may also ask for a shorter repayment term or a co-signer.

On the other hand, a credit score of 700 or higher is usually seen as good, and the borrower may be able to get a lower interest rate. This means that they will pay less in interest over the life of the loan.

Outstanding scores are those of 800 or more. Each lender has its own range of credit scores, but the FICO Score range is often used.

- **Excellent:** 800–850
- **Very Good:** 740–799
- **Good:** 670–739
- **Fair**: 580–669
- **Poor:** 300–579

A person's credit score may also affect how much of a down payment they need to get a smartphone, cable service, or utilities or to rent an apartment. Also, lenders check people's credit scores all the time, especially when deciding whether to change a credit card's interest rate or credit limit.

How Your Score Is Calculated

Equifax, Experian, and TransUnion are the three main credit reporting companies in the United States. They keep consumer credit histories up to date and record new information about them. Even though the three credit bureaus may collect different kinds of information, there are five main things that are used to make a credit score:

1. Payment history
2. Total amount owed
3. Length of credit history
4. Types of credit
5. New credit

Three-fifths of a person's credit score comes from their payment history, which shows if they pay their bills on time. It takes into account how much of a person's available credit is being used, which is called credit utilization. The total amount owed makes up 30% of the total amount owed. Credit history length is worth 15%. People with longer credit histories are thought to be less risky because there is more information to look at when figuring out payment history.

Ten percent of a person's credit score is based on the type of credit they use. This shows whether they use installment credit, like car or home loans, or revolving credit, like credit cards. Ten percent comes from new credit, which looks at how many new accounts a person has, how many new accounts they recently applied for, which led to credit checks, and when their most recent account opened.

FICO Score – Popular Credit Scoring Model

The FICO credit score was made by the Fair Isaac Corporation (FICO). Lenders look at borrowers' FICO scores and other information on their credit reports to decide if they are a good credit risk and should give them credit. FICO scores use information from five areas to determine a person's creditworthiness: payment history, current amount of debt, types of credit used, length of credit history, and new credit accounts.

FICO Score Ranges

The full range of FICO scores is from 300 to 850. Credit scores between 670 and 739 usually mean that your credit history is "excellent," which is what most lenders would want. On the other hand, people who borrow between 580 and 669 may have trouble getting loans at good rates.

Lenders look at more than just a borrower's FICO score to decide if they are creditworthy. They look at things like income, length of employment, and the type of credit sought.

Calculating FICO Scores

FICO figures out credit scores by giving each factor a different amount of weight for each person. Payment history, on the other hand, makes up 35% of the score. Accounts that are still open make up 30%, the length of the credit history 15%, new credit accounts 10%, and the mix of credit accounts 10%.

These are the main things that make up a FICO score:

Payment History (35%)

Your credit card payment history shows that you always pay your bills on time. Credit reports show how much you've paid on each line of credit, as well as any bankruptcy or collection issues and payments that were late or not made at all.

Accounts Owed (30%)

The amount of money that someone owes is called their "accounts owing."

Having a lot of debt doesn't always mean you have bad credit. Instead, FICO looks at how much debt there is compared to how much credit is available. Someone who owes $10,000 but has all of their credit lines fully extended and all of their credit cards maxed out might have a lower credit score than someone who owes $100,000 but doesn't have any accounts close to the limit.

Length of Credit History (15%)

Most of the time, a person's credit score goes up as time goes on. A person with a short credit history may still have a high credit score if they have good scores in other areas as well. The oldest account age, the youngest account age, and the overall average are all parts of FICO scores.

Credit Mix (10%)

There are a lot of accounts, which is the credit mix. For people to have good credit, they need to have a variety of accounts, including checking and savings accounts, credit cards, installment loans (like auto or signature loans), and mortgages.

New Credit (10%)

When you open a new account, that account is called "new credit." When someone opens a lot of new accounts quickly, it shows that they are a risky borrower and lowers their credit score.

FICO Score	Rating	What the Score Means
<580	Poor	❖ Well Below Average ❖ Demonstrates you to lenders as a risky borrower
<580-669	Fair	❖ Below average ❖ Many lenders will approve loans
670-739	Good	❖ Near or will consider this a good score ❖ Most lenders consider this a good score
740-799	Very Good	❖ Above average ❖ Demonstrates you to lenders as a dependable borrower
800+	Exceptional	❖ Well above average ❖ Demonstrate to lenders you're an exceptional borrower
		❖

What Can Hurt Your Credit Score

The information about your finances in your credit report is turned into a number that is your credit score. These are the three companies that offer credit reports: Equifax, Experian, and TransUnion. Other businesses and creditors send in financial information about you and your customers to help get a good picture of how creditworthy you are.

Some creditors report to all three agencies, and creditors only report to one. A scoring algorithm looks through the information in your credit report to find your credit score. There are other ways to figure out your credit score, but lenders and credit card companies mostly use the FICO score. A creditor will look at both your credit report and credit score to decide if they can trust you when you apply for a loan or credit card. Based on that and other financial information, they'll decide if you can get a loan or credit card. Bad credit means you will pay more in interest if you do get a loan. This is because lenders think you are more likely to not pay if you have a bad credit history.

You can get the best terms and conditions if you have good credit. Obviously, if you want to keep your interest rates low, you need to have the best credit report and score possible. In other words, what is on your credit report, and how does it affect your credit score? This is how everything turns out.

Payment History

The most important thing that determines your credit score is how well you pay your bills on time every month. It makes up 35% of your score. It comes from accounts you've had in the last seven years and will show up on your credit report. You can see how much you've paid each month for a long time on any loan, credit card, or mortgage.

It will also show you how much you owe each month. If you pay your cell phone company or utility company late, they may report it, but when you pay them on time, they rarely do.

If you are behind on any payments, they will show how long they were late, which could be 30 to 150 days (or more if the account went into default). If you don't pay on time, your credit score will go down.

Total Debt

Thirty percent of your FICO score is based on how much debt you have. Your revolving debt, like credit cards, is very important. Installment debts, like a mortgage or school loan, aren't as important. Lenders look at your debt-to-credit ratio, which shows how much you owe compared to your credit card's maximum credit limit. This is also called "credit usage."

If you're drawing too much on your credit cards, your credit score will go down. If two people have the same amount of debt but different maximum amounts, their ratings could be very different. This is because the ratio is based on amounts. A person whose credit card limit is $10,000 and has $3,000 charged on it has a debt-to-credit ratio of only 30%.

If someone charged $3,000 on a card with a $5,000 limit, on the other hand, they would have a 60% ratio and, all other things being equal, a much lower credit score.

Length of Credit History

Fifteen percent of your credit score is based on how long you've had credit. This is because a lender can't tell if you can or want to pay back a loan if you don't have a history of doing so. How long you've had your loans, credit cards, and other accounts open is part of the scoring formula.

Rent payments aren't usually part of a person's FICO score, which is a shame. However, some credit bureaus offer a rental reporting service that you could use as extra proof on your credit application.

New Credit

Another part of your credit report that you will look at is inquiries. This is about any credit applications you've made in the last two years, and it could lower your credit score by 10%. Each inquiry will lose about five points in the first year unless several are made about the same product within a few weeks of each other. It only means that you were looking at rates for a loan or credit card, and it is usually a single inquiry.

Credit Mix

The last 10 percent of your credit score is based on the types of credit you have. We already told you that revolving credit, like credit cards and store cards, is worse for your credit score than installment loans. This is because most loans are backed by something of value, like a house or car. This shows that you have something valuable and are more committed to paying back your debts than to making purchases with a credit card that you don't know about. Also, student loans are more popular than credit cards because they are an investment in your future ability to make money, and the faster you make money, the faster you can pay off your debts.

Negative Items on Your Credit Report

The Fair Credit Reporting Act (FCRA) limits how long a credit bureau can keep negative information on your report. On the other hand, neutral and positive information is usually kept for life. Also, over time, each bad item does less and less damage to your score. The short answer is that your bad credit won't last forever as long as you start doing some good things. Also, bad things can be officially erased from your report before the usual deadline, though this may not always be possible depending on your situation. You can also choose to spend more time getting rid of new negative things instead of older ones since they fall off faster.

Here is a list of the different types of bad things that might be on your credit report, along with how long they will stay there if you don't try to get them taken off.

Fees and Charges

A charge-off is when a creditor decides they can't collect on a debt. They might take it off their list of past-due accounts that can be reported instead of marking it as overdue or past-due. When the debt is charged off, the company's accounts receivable report looks better, but that doesn't mean the debt is gone. The people who buy debts pay very little for them compared to the amount they are owed.

Once the debt buyer has bought the debt, they can try to get the full amount owed plus court costs, interest, late fees, and other penalties by calling the debtor and taking them to court for the full amount plus any fees that are due. Charge-offs can stay on your credit report for up to seven years and 180 days after the due date.

Collections: It's tricky with collections because paying them off could hurt your credit score because the start date is reset to when the debt was reported. Before taking action on collections, read on must figure out how to get through these dangerous waters.

Like charge-offs, collection accounts can be kept for up to seven years after the date you fell behind on your original debt.

Paying late fees

Your credit bureau may report any payment that is more than 30 days late, even if you finally make the payment on time. Some creditors, on the other hand, don't let the debtor know about the late payment until a second payment is due. This is because they don't want to upset good customers who just missed the due date and paid it back the next month. Credit reporting rules say that after the second missed payment, all past-due payments must be reported.

Accounts that are past due or late payments can be marked as such for up to seven years after the last due date.

Bankruptcies

Records of bankruptcies can only be kept for 10 years from the date they were filed. The ten-year period starts on the date your case was thrown out if it was. How you file for bankruptcy can also change the length of time. 7 bankruptcies are kept on file for 10 years, but 13 bankruptcies are kept on file for only seven years.

Foreclosures: As well, foreclosures can be kept for up to seven years. Luckily, you won't have to wait nearly as long to buy a new home once your finances are back on track. You could get a mortgage in as little as two years, but it could take longer if you want a different type of loan.

Judgments

As long as the case was filed more than seven years ago or until the applicable statute of limitations runs out, the judgment can be kept. Most statutes of limitations are less than seven years, so that's how long it's likely to stay on your credit report after a lawsuit or judgment. Check the laws in your state to be sure.

Repossessions

For up to seven years, repossessions can also be kept track of. Keep in mind that even after the property (like a car) has been taken away, you are still responsible for paying off any debt, even if it doesn't show up on your credit report.

Tax Bonds

Federal law says that tax liens that you haven't paid can stay on your credit report forever. Credit bureaus may get rid of them after about ten years, though. Paid tax liens can stay on your record for up to seven years after they are paid off.

Chapter 03: Credit Repairing

Introduction to Credit Repair

If someone has bad credit, they can fix it. This is called "credit repair." It's possible that all you have to do to fix your credit is dispute false information with the credit bureaus. If you need to fix your credit after identity theft, it could cost a lot.

Another way to fix credit is to deal with underlying money problems, like not having a budget, and start to address lenders' real concerns.

How Credit Repair Works

There are many companies that say they can help fix wrong information that may be on your credit report it takes time and work. Credit bureaus can't delete information that was sent by a third party. Instead, the details can be disputed if they were not told correctly or were wrong. Credit repair companies might look into these things, but the person being evaluated might do it, too. Everyone can get a free credit report from each of the three main credit bureaus once a year, and every time, information in their report is used against them in a bad way, like being turned down for credit.

If there are mistakes or missing information on a person's credit report, they may want to dispute it. How well someone can rebuild and fix their credit may depend on more than just how accurate the information is or how quickly fraud is found. It may also depend on how they use and interact with their credit.

A person's payment history may have a big effect on their credit score. A person can raise their credit score by making sure their payments are on time or by changing how they pay for credit that they still owe. The amount of credit the person uses may also play a role. To give you an example, if someone is using a lot of their available credit and making the minimum payments on time, the amount of debt they have could hurt their credit score.

The problem is that the sum of the debts owed to them may make it hard for them to make quick cash payments. Getting rid of some of their debt might help them improve their credit score.

The DIY Method for Credit Repair

It's possible to work on improving your credit on your own, even if you have some bad things on it. First, though, read up on the Fair Credit Reporting Act (FCRA) to know what rights you have when dealing with credit bureaus, lenders, and even debt collectors. Follow these step-by-step instructions to learn how to find bad things on your credit report, like late payments, loans that are past due, and other things. This will give you the best chance of getting them removed.

Step 1: get a copy of your credit report.

You should have already looked at your Equifax, Experian, and TransUnion credit reports. If you haven't already, this is the first thing you need to do. It's free and easy to do at AnnualCreditReport.com. You can get all three reports in just a few minutes after giving your personal information and answering a few security questions to make sure you're who you say you are. You can also ask for hard copies to be sent to you if you want to. You could also call 1-877-322-8228.

Step 2: The second step is to carefully read each report.

When you get your credit reports, you should check them again to make sure they are correct. Remember that your three credit reports are not always the same, as some lenders and creditors only report to one or two of them. One of the credit bureaus may have the wrong information about your finances, even if they report to all three. Don't just assume that the information is the same on all three; carefully read each one.

So, what do you want to find? To begin, make sure that your basic personal information is correct and that your report does not list anyone else. Then, read each page carefully and make sure you understand what this page is about. From the start date of your account to the biggest amount you've ever had, make a note of any parts that don't seem right, especially if there's a bad item like a late payment. You should also make sure that you are the owner of each credit line to make sure that no one else has opened an account in your name without your permission.

After looking over all of your open and closed credit accounts, pay attention to the part of your report that says you have bad credit. This is where it lists all of your accounts that you haven't paid on time, collections, or public records.

These things will hurt your score the most and should probably be at the top of your list of things to get rid of.

Step 3: File a dispute and ask that negative items be taken off.

If you find any wrong, late, misleading, biased, incomplete, or questionable information on your credit report, you have the right and duty to dispute it and have it taken off. Also, getting rid of negative things could have a big positive effect on your credit scores. A lot of people still don't know that they can be erased, but every day, thousands of people successfully dispute these items with credit bureaus. That's not as hard as you think, and it's a much better choice than waiting years for bad marks to go away from your credit report.

First, send a certified letter to the credit bureau describing the bad thing. You can find examples of letters of disagreement here. You should make a copy for yourself and make sure to choose return receipt so you know they got your letter.

After that, the credit bureau has 30 days to answer your question. Some people may say that you can dispute online, but we've found that customers have a lot more success disputing by mail. Check out

Why You Should Never Dispute Credit Report Errors Online for more information.

In your letter, make sure to list all the wrong things that are on your credit report. Don't send the originals of any supporting documents; instead, send copies. That being said, supporting documents are not needed. Don't forget that credit bureaus have to show proof.

Also, put in your name, phone number, and current address. Stay polite and professional, and don't add your own thoughts or opinions.

You can either explain why you don't agree with the bad item or just say that you don't agree with it. If you want to dispute something, the law says that you have to ask about it, and the creditor must show proof that the item is correct. You might have to go back and forth between lenders and credit bureaus more than once. It might take some work and time, but it might be worth it for your credit score.

What Can You Do to Improve a Bad Credit

- By law, you have the right to correct any inaccurate information in your credit bureau.
- If a lender rejects your application due to negative information in your credit report, you must identify the relevant credit bureau.
- Upon request, the credit bureau must disclose the contents of your credit report, and if done within 30 days of a refusal, the service will not be billed.
- Ensure the information on your credit report is correct and complete.
- Under the Fair Credit Reporting Act, you have the right to challenge the completeness or accuracy of your account information.
- Inform the credit bureau in writing why you believe the information is inaccurate when disputing the information.

- If the dispute is not frivolous or irrelevant, the credit bureau should reconsider the matter and correct any inaccuracies.
- Information that cannot be verified should be deleted by the credit bureau.
- If you disagree with the results of a credit bureau investigation, you can file a brief protest statement, and the credit bureau will include your dispute in future reports upon request.
- Negative information in your credit report, if correct, can only be removed over time. Bankruptcy information can be reported for ten years, and other harmful data for seven years.
- Credit bureaus are legally allowed to report bankruptcy for ten years and other harmful data for seven years.
- No action can be taken to request the removal of correct information from your credit report until the reporting period has expired.
- Be cautious of ads promising to "fix" or "clean up" bad credit, judgments, or bankruptcy, as they can rarely deliver on such promises.

Credit Repair Service Companies

Your credit score is a big part of figuring out the interest rate on your mortgage and other loan terms you will be given when you buy a house. If your credit score is low, a credit repair company might be able to help you raise it.

As an alternative, you could hire a credit repair company to talk to credit bureaus on your behalf. They will fix your credit report and get rid of the mistakes and bad things that have been hurting it if you pay them.

Naturally, you have the right to dispute any false information that has been spread about you. Nevertheless, a lot of people need help with this because they think the work is too hard.

How Credit Repair Services Works

You will get a copy of your credit report from all three major credit bureaus (Experian®, Equifax®, and TransUnion®) as the first thing a credit repair service does. They will be looking through your report for any claims that aren't true or are harmful.

Credit repair services can help you fix mistakes that aren't true on your credit report, but they can't lie on your behalf. The company will call the credit bureaus or data providers that gave them your information after looking over your credit report. A lot of these groups not only help people who have been scammed with credit cards, but they also keep an eye on your credit report to stop identity theft.

Ways to Evaluate Credit Repair Companies

If you can't pay your bills, you might be tempted to call a business that says it can help you settle your debts. This kind of company might offer "secured" debt consolidation loans, debt counseling, or debt reorganization plans that stop creditors from trying to collect your debt. Before you sign up with that company:

Investigate thoroughly.

It is important that you know what the business does and how much it costs. Don't count on promises made over the phone that aren't written down in your contract. Get in touch with the Better Business Bureau and the consumer protection office in your area. They might be able to tell you if other customers have signed up to say bad things about the deal. When people ask these companies for help, they sometimes give them more problems.

Some big short-term loans, like debt consolidation, may have high hidden costs, and your home may need them as insurance. A dishonest company can change the terms of these loans, and if they do, you could lose your home. Companies that help people with debt or reorganization may charge a lot of money or a percentage of your debt, but they won't do what they say they will do. Some can do a little more than just tell people who are in debt about a bankruptcy lawyer who charges extra fees.

Companies that offer debt relief or reorganization plans may not say that debt adjustment is a type of bankruptcy. You must have a steady source of income and a payment plan for your creditors that the bankruptcy court will accept in order to be eligible.

Bankruptcy companies might not tell you everything you need to know or help you through what can be a hard and time-consuming legal process. Debt problems are annoying, but be careful about what you do to fix them. Some "solutions" will make things worse.

Quick Tips for Repairing Your Credit

Getting negative information taken off your credit report can have a big effect on your score, but the process takes a lot of time. You can still try a few things if you want to see results right away. Read through the whole list to see which ones you can start doing right away to improve your credit. Some are small fixes, while others could have a big impact.

Cut down on how much credit you use.

Remember the credit usage ratio we talked about before? If you use all of your credit cards, your credit score will go down. If you pay off your credit card debt, your ratio will go down, and your score will go up. Focus on cards with high balances instead of cards with low balances. This could lead to a 100-point rise over a few months.

Ask your credit card company to raise your limit.

To lower your credit utilization, you don't have to pay off more debt. You can still make progress. It's possible that you can get your credit limit raised by calling more than one credit card company. You don't want to be charged more than what you owe. Instead, you want a higher limit so that the amount you owe now is a smaller part of the credit you have available. Let me show you an example. Take the case where you owe $5,000 on a $10,000 credit card. You'd spend half of your credit. However, if you raised your limit to $15,000, the $5,000 you had would only make up 33% of your new maximum.

It helps to have a history of making payments on time with your creditors before calling them. They will probably value your loyalty as a customer enough to give you more credit.

Get authorized to use this site.

It takes time to build credit, but there is a way to make the process go faster. Make sure the person you want to add as an authorized user has good credit. This could be a close friend or family member. Your credit report will show that credit card account right away. There is some risk in this choice: if your friend or family member doesn't pay or holds on to a large amount, that will show up on your credit report as a bad entry. The other person's credit will also suffer if you borrow too much money and don't make any payments that you are supposed to make. This could be a great plan, but it needs to be used carefully.

Get rid of all your credit card debt at once

Getting a debt consolidation loan is another easy way to improve your credit. You use it to pay off your credit cards and then make one monthly payment on the loan. It's basically a personal loan. Getting a lower loan rate might help you save money on your monthly payments if your credit card interest rates are high. By getting pre-approved, you can compare rates from different cards and see what kinds of rates you can get. Installment loans are better for your credit score than revolving credit, so even if you pay your bills on time every month, it will still be better.

For better credit, get a loan.

Credit-builder loans are often available from smaller banks and credit unions to help people fix their credit. You don't have access to the money that is put into your account when you apply for a loan. After that, you begin paying back the loan every month. After you've paid back the loan in full, you can use the money.

It may seem strange to pay back money you can't even spend, but it's a way for the bank to feel safe while you show them you're a responsible borrower. When you make your payments on time and get the money, the bank tells the credit bureaus about it. This is good for your credit score.

Chapter 04: Credit Boosting

How to Increase Your Credit Score by Removing Negative Items

For those who can't get negative items taken off their credit report or would rather wait for them to slowly fade away, you may still be able to raise their credit score. It's also important to be careful when handling collections so that you don't reset the statute of limitations by accident. As part of your overall plan to fix your credit, make sure you follow these steps to make the most of all your opportunities and avoid unintended setbacks that could have long-lasting effects.

Look over your accounts in collections.

Start by going over your newest collections. They have the most impact on your credit score because newer debt is given more weight. Think about the type of loan you're paying back as well.

Medical debt doesn't hurt your credit score as much as other types of debt, so pay off your other debts first. If you can, make full payments on time because making partial payments could reset the time limit on how long those accounts can stay on your credit report.

You could also try to strike a deal with the debt collectors so that you pay less than you owe. Just remember that you might have to report the amount you were denied as income on your tax return. This could mean more taxes and maybe even a higher tax rate if it puts you in a higher tax band.

When the debt collector acts like you haven't paid at all, that's another problem with debt collection. Make sure you have written agreements for payments and keep copies of all your account paperwork to avoid this kind of fraud.

Keep an eye on your credit report.

Once you've taken care of your collections accounts, check your credit report again to make sure that the changes are shown correctly. Check your credit report and score again in a few weeks. The accounts may not be gone for a month or two. You could file a dispute with the credit bureau if you don't see any improvements or if the negative item stays on your report. As long as you keep good records, you should have all the paperwork you need to settle the dispute quickly.

The Most Effective Ways to Boost Your Credit Score

Because of how credit scores are calculated, some of the things you do will have a bigger effect on your score than others. Generally, the best way to improve your score is to pay your bills on time and handle your money properly. When you borrow a reasonable amount of money and can easily pay it back, it shows lenders that you are responsible for your money and won't lose it. The first two tips will, without a doubt, help you improve your credit score.

On time, pay your bills.

If you want to improve your credit score, all you have to do is pay your bills on time. Even though this seems ridiculously easy, it works because nothing shows lenders that you don't take your debts seriously, like a history of paying on time. Every lender wants to be paid on time and in full.

Avoid Getting Too Much Credit

A bigger credit risk comes from having a lot of lines of credit or big debts. This is because you're close to "overextending your credit." This just means that you'll be taking on more debt than you can easily pay back.

Banks know that you will have a harder time paying off your debts if you have a lot of debt, even though you are currently paying your bills on time.

Pay off your debts.

Your credit score will go down if you have a lot of debt. For example, if your credit card has a $1,000 limit and you usually have a $900 balance on it, lenders will see you as a lower credit risk than someone with the same credit card account but a balance of $100 or less. If you really want to raise your credit score, you should start by paying down your biggest debt. This will make it less of a burden on your overall credit score.

Have different kinds of credit.

One thing that goes into figuring out your credit score is the types of credit you have. Most of the time, lenders want to see that you can handle different types of credit well. It's better to have more than one type of credit and pay them off on time. For example, credit cards are a type of personal credit, while a mortgage or car loan is a larger type of credit.

Do not let your credit score drop.

If your credit score is lower than you'd like, it's probably because of a small mistake or oversight you made with money in the past. Not everyone with bad credit has a low credit score because of something they did. Bad people can sometimes try to steal your credit card. Here are some ways to protect yourself and your credit from people who want to steal it online or off of you:

Watch out for fraud

A lot of people who pay their bills on time and don't owe much money are surprised to learn that they have low credit scores every year. A lot of the time, this is caused by fraud.

Some people steal your personal information and use it to pretend to be you in order to get into your accounts or steal your identity. This is called fraud.

Practice Safe Computing, Banking, and Safe Business

To stay safe from fraud, always follow secure banking and financial practices:

1. **Keep account numbers and PINs safe:** Keep your account and ID numbers safe when you use debit at the store, and never give your PIN to anyone. Do not write down your PIN or account numbers. You do not know when someone could get this information wrong.

2. **Only do business with whom you trust:** You should shred the credit card applications and letters that come with them before throwing them away if you get "pre-approved" credit card applications in the mail. Most of the time, this is not paranoid. Identity thieves will sometimes carry trash to find these forms and fill them out so they can steal your identity.

3. **Computer Skills:** Install a good firewall and antivirus protection system on your computer and make sure you keep it up to date. It's even better to take a safe computing class at a college or civic center near you. There are many helpful tips that will help you keep your data safe while you're online.

4. **Buying Concern:** Do not buy anything online from a company that you do not trust or that does not have encryption technology and a clear privacy policy. Also, never use open-end credit to pay for things online; always use a credit card.

5. Open-end credit doesn't protect you as much as credit cards do. It is not your money that is stolen if your card information is stolen while you are shopping online. It is your credit. If someone uses your card without your permission, you can only fight to get charges taken off of your MasterCard. If you have

open-end credit, your real money could be taken, and you'll have to fight for months to get it back.

6. **Aware of intruders**: No matter how careful you are with your computer; you should never send private information through email or your computer. If you get an email from your bank asking you to click on a link to confirm your information, be very careful. This is a common scam that comes from criminals or hackers, not your bank. You need to get in touch with your company or banks right away.

7. **Be attentive to unknown emails, ads, or phone calls:** Most of them are from real businesses, but some will call you and say they can give you a credit card, but then they'll charge your real card without sending you anything.

8. **Be wary of offers that appear too good to be true:** If someone offers you a free high-tech computer in exchange for your account information and a ten-million-dollar check, you should think twice before sending them your money and information.

9. **Good offers are always best:** Scammers often take advantage of your trust in others and your desire to make money. People who do these things count on you getting so excited about certain products or services that you won't think straight. Show them they're wrong. If someone makes an offer that seems too good to be true, you should look into it online, call the Better Business Bureau, or ask the person making the offer some questions. If someone gives you a suggestion without asking for it, don't tell anyone else about it until both the company and the person giving you the suggestion check it out.

10. **Read the fine print**: It's possible for some services or businesses to have a small print in their contract or agreement that lets them charge you extra fees or take back an offer. Always read the small print when you get a suggestion in the mail or by email.

11. **Be alert for a sudden interruption in your email or phone**: After a few tries, if you still haven't gotten your mail, call the post office and ask if your address has been recent "change of address." It's true, even though it sounds weird.

Check Your Credit Score Regularly

If you check your credit score every day or at least once a year, three times a year is better. This way, you are more likely to notice problems and errors. Also, make sure you check your credit score with each company. Report anything strange or unfamiliar right away, like a credit account you probably didn't open.

These mistakes are sometimes caused by mistakes at the agency, but they could also mean that someone is using your identity.

Why Your Credit History Is Important

The reasons why credit history holds crucial importance are being stated below:

- Creditors consider various factors for credit decisions, with a significant reliance on credit history.
- Most creditors obtain credit history reports from local credit bureaus to assess past credit management.
- Credit bureaus collect and sell consumer credit information, serving as the primary source for credit history details.
- Credit bureau accounts are based on information provided to creditors over time, including residence, employment, and public domain issues like lawsuits or bankruptcy.
- Reports track payments on credit cards, installment loans, and other credit accounts, aiding creditors in assessing credit risk.
- Timely payments on loans enhance the likelihood of obtaining additional credit.
- Some creditors may be hesitant to extend credit to individuals without established records with other creditors.

- Borrowers with a history of late payments, property recovery, lawsuits, or bankruptcy may face challenges in obtaining consumer loans.
- Be cautious of ads promising "current credit cards" or "major credit cards" regardless of credit history, as legitimate creditors prioritize assessing credit risk.
- Qualifications meeting credit criteria are essential for loan approval; premature certainty is challenging to achieve.

How to Establish a Credit History and Establish Creditworthiness

It's very important to build a good credit history. Setting up your first credit account can take a lot of time if you don't know much about your credit history. It's a problem for both young people just starting out in their careers and older people who have never used credit.

Also, it affects people who are divorced or widowed and have joint accounts payable that are only listed in the names of their spouses. Get in touch with your local credit bureau if you don't know what's on your report. In most cities, you can find two or three credit bureaus in the Yellow Pages under "Credit" or "Credit bureaus." You can pay a small fee and get a copy of your credit report. They will tell you what information is kept on file.

If you had credit in the past under a different name or address and it's not on your report, you can ask the credit bureau to add it. If you split the bills with your ex-spouse, ask the credit bureau to add them to your report, too. There is no rule that says credit bureaus have to add new accounts to your file, but many will for a small fee.

Finally, if you and your spouse share a credit account, make sure the lender reports it under both of your names. Creditors don't have to give credit bureaus information about your account history.

But let's say the creditor declares the invoice. Then, either both spouses can use the invoice or are legally bound to pay it back. In this case, the Equal Opportunities Act lets you ask the creditor to report the information under both names. If you want to get in touch with your lender or credit bureau faster, please write it down and include important details like account numbers. Make sure you keep a copy of everything you send for business reasons. You should start building your credit history if you don't already have one. You could get a loan from a local business, like a department store, if you have a steady income and have lived in the same area for at least a year. You can also borrow a small amount from a bank or credit union where you have a checking or savings account.

A local bank or department store might give you a loan even if it doesn't meet the requirements of big lenders. Before you apply for a loan, find out if the lender sends information about your credit history to the credit bureaus in your area. Some creditors don't do it, but most do. Suppose you can try to get a loan that lets you enroll. It helps your credit score. If you don't get the loan, find out why.

There could be more than one reason besides not having a credit history. Your income might not be enough to meet the minimum needs of your creditors, or you might not have worked hard enough at your current job. Things can get better with time. You can apply again after your pay goes up, or you can go to a different lender right away. To be safe, though, you should wait at least six months between requests. Credit bureaus keep track of all the requests they get about you.

Some lenders might say no to your request if they think you want to open too many new accounts too quickly. You can get someone with good credit to cosign with you if you still can't get credit. Being able to get a loan with a co-signer is much more likely because they promise to pay if you don't. Try to get a loan on your own again after you pay off the debt.

How to Maintain Your Credit Health Over Time

You should be able to look forward after taking care of all the problems in your past that are affecting your credit now. You can keep your better credit score and avoid going back to bad habits by following these tips.

Hold on to your money.

Living within your means is one of the most important things you can do to keep your credit and money in good shape. Make sure you save some money every month, even if you're good at getting your paychecks to go further. You never know when you might need it. Do not charge things you don't need to your credit card because it makes it harder to keep track of how much you're spending. Instead, check your bank account every night to see how things are going, or only use cash to avoid buying things you don't need.

On time, pay your bills.

Thanks for the information. Your credit score is mostly based on how quickly you pay your bills every month, especially those that will send the information to credit bureaus. You could see a big drop in your credit score after just one late payment.

Get out your calendar and start putting due dates into groups. This way, you'll know exactly what you owe every month. If you need more help, set up automatic payments through your bank.

Be smart about how you use a secured credit card.

Once you have a plan for your monthly spending, you should think about getting a credit card to improve your credit score. If you have trouble getting approved for one, try getting a secured credit card. It was made especially for people who are rebuilding their credit. You put down a security deposit equal to your credit limit. That money doesn't go toward your monthly payment; it's just there as security until you start making payments on time. You could begin with a $500 limit and gradually raise it until you no longer need the secured card at all. In the meantime, you'll start a new history of making payments that are reported every month.

Chapter 05: Money Management Tactics

Introduction to Money Management

Money management means doing something planned and smart with your money so that you can use your assets in the best way possible. Activities like budgeting, saving, managing debt, investing, and more could be added. Managing your money means making smart choices about your money. The better you are at managing your money, the smarter your choices will be.

Money Management Goals

If you're not sure why you should care about managing your money, let's start with the big picture. Money management that is smart can help you reach many financial and personal goals, such as:

- ✓ Confidently affording your daily needs
- ✓ Being able to spend on fun things
- ✓ Buying big-ticket items, like a home or dream vacation
- ✓ Providing for your children or family members
- ✓ Being able to retire comfortably
- ✓ Donating to causes you care about

More than anything else, knowing how to handle your money well may give you peace of mind about your finances.

Money Management Principles

Even though there are a lot of different ways to handle your money, these basic rules will help you sort through them all and focus on what's most important for your financial health.

1. Know which way your money is going.

Knowing about your money can be scary, but it gives you power. When you look at your personal snapshot, you're not supposed to judge yourself or berate yourself for mistakes you've made with your money. It's just a great chance to look at everything that's going on in your life and figure out what to do next.

So, write down how much you earn and spend each month, how much you have saved and invested, how much debt you have (like credit cards or other loans), and anything else that affects your financial picture. Doing this just once is a great way to find ways to make things better, but keeping an eye on it all the time through budgeting is even better. (I'll say more about this soon.)

2. You should try to live within your means and stay out of debt.

One of the most basic rules of money management is never to spend more than you earn. You want to make sure that your monthly expenses don't go over your monthly income. This isn't always possible because you may need to borrow money for big purchases or emergencies.

It's very important to stress that you should use your net income, which is your income after taxes, to figure this out. You will spend more than you earn if you only use your basic salary because you won't include tax money that will never make it to your bank account. Again, making a budget can be a great way to figure out how much you can spend and stick to it.

3. Pay off as much debt as you can

When you get your finances under control, one of the first things you should do is pay off all of your debts as soon as possible. This is because the interest on your debts costs you money every month.

Long-term debt for big purchases, like a mortgage or school loans, is a different story. You may just pay those off when the installments are due. Look at any debt you have, like credit card balances that are past due, and come up with a plan to pay it off. Some people choose one of two ways:

- ✓ **Snowball method:** Sort your debts by how much they cost and pay the smallest amounts first. Then, pay the bare minimum on the larger amounts.

- ✓ **Avalanche method:** Sort your loans by interest rate (APR), from highest to lowest. Pay the loan with the highest APR first, and only make the minimum payments on the others.

4. Put Money Aside (and Have Some Fun)

Once you've made good progress on paying off your debts, you should start saving any extra cash for later use. Beginning to save for the following things in this order:

- **Save for unexpected expenses with an emergency fund:** In the event of an accident, emergency, or job loss, this can help you stay out of debt. As a general rule, you should save three to six months' worth of income.

- **Save for the future with a retirement account:** In the event of an accident, emergency, or job loss, this can help you stay out of debt. As a general rule, you should save three to six months' worth of income.

Save for fun and personal financial goals: Don't forget to set aside some money for yourself. Set up a savings account to work toward big financial goals, like going on a dream vacation or buying a house one day.

According to the 70/30 rule, you should try to spend 70% of your income on necessities and save 30%. The 70/20/10 rule goes even further, saying that you should save 20% and use the other 10% for gifts or extra debt payments. But the truth is that any amount you can save every month will help, and it may add up quickly.

5. Invest to Keep Growing Your Money

The money you've saved up might be worth investing if you want it to make more money for you. Your money may grow a lot over time because of the interest you earn on it, even if you don't do anything.

Putting your money into investments comes with some risk, so make sure you save enough for both regular expenses and an emergency fund. Then, for the rest, start making a good plan for investing. For starters, you can learn how to start here.

The Critical Importance of Saving

Saving money is an important part of being a good teen with money, but your teen might not find it easy. Next time your teen asks why they need to save money, give them one of these reasons.

1. Having more control when you save money

Kids want more and more power as they get older. And by the time they are teenagers? They not only want it, they make it happen.

Power over what they wear. Choice over when they have to spend time with their families. The food they eat is up to them. Control over the people they hang out with.

Talk to your teen about the idea that giving them more control over their money will motivate them to save it. Think of a river as the flow of money in your life; it's always going by you.

2. Putting money away will help you have more fun in your 20s.

To be honest, there is enough fun to be had in your twenties. It's exciting to have more rights, responsibilities, and duties as an adult. Not having any cash on hand. OR not having enough money to live on your parent's couch or in their old room.

That is not good for your kid. They should not have a great chance that they can only take if they have some money saved.

For example:

- ✓ Study abroad opportunity
- ✓ Job break with a move involved
- ✓ Spring break trip with college friends
- ✓ Etc.

3. Teens Need an Emergency Fund, Too

Your teen might not know what an emergency savings fund is. It's a type of savings account where you keep money that you should only use in an emergency. This doesn't mean they can't have one, though.

As a child enter adolescence, they are given more responsibilities and more adult-like belongings that need adult-like money to fix and maintain.

A teenager might need an emergency fund to:

- ✓ Spend money on a car repair (flat tire, failed inspection issues, car accident costs, etc.)
- ✓ You have to pay for lost school property. For example, I lost a $328 band tunic and had to pay for it myself. It hurt to write that check when I was 17 years old.
- ✓ Random data overages cost money that wasn't planned for!
- ✓ They are stuck because they don't know how to handle their money or their adult responsibilities.

4. Parents Won't Be Paying for Everything Anymore

At some point, you may have already done this, but you will stop letting your teen know about some things. You should talk to your 18-year-old, 22-year-old, etc. if not your teen.

This point has to do with it. They will need to save money since you, as a parent, won't be willing to pay for everything anymore.

They may be required to pay for the following financial obligations:

- ✓ Plan for Smartphone Data
- ✓ Car insurance and gas
- ✓ Weekend buddy gatherings
- ✓ Vending machine excursions after school
- ✓ Vehicle maintenance
- ✓ Non-school uniform/additional clothing, etc.

5. People Like to Help People who are Helping Themselves

Now is a great time to tell your teen that other people, including you, are more likely to want to help them if they help themselves. In this case, they could help themselves by saving money toward a savings goal or building up an emergency fund.

6. As You Get Older, You Gain Both Rights AND Responsibilities

Teenage years and early adulthood are exciting and scary times with lots of choices your teen has never even thought of. With all of their new adult rights and privileges come new responsibilities. We want the best for them, but we also want to make sure they are ready for them. Tell your child that having rights means having responsibilities, like paying for things.

They can work from anywhere, live anywhere, and date anyone they want. Their nights out will be endless.

7. Because credit cards are a poor backup plan

In the back of their mind, your child may be thinking that they can always use a credit card if they spend too much or need money quickly (inspiring them to continue with their current, no-saving-money behaviors). That being said, there is a big difference here. Adults are more likely to have established credit, which means they can do things like raise their credit limit in case of an emergency or even have a credit card.

Tips for Saving Money

If your child thinks about it, they might always have a credit card on hand in case they spend too much or need cash quickly (inspiring them to continue with their current, no-saving-money behaviors). Still, this is very different. People who are adults are more likely to have established credit. This means that they can do things like get a credit card or raise their credit limit in case of an emergency.

Keep track of how much you spend.

You might be able to make the necessary changes if you know where your money is going. For one or two weeks, use BALANCE's Fritter Finder tool to keep track of how much you spend.

Keep needs and wants separate.

Is that 42-inch flat-screen TV really something you need? In times when money is tight, only spend what you need to.

It's not smart to use credit to pay off debts.

In the short term, using credit may make things easier, but in the long run, it may make your monthly bills go up.

Always save.

You can have money automatically moved from your checking account to your savings account every month, or you can have some of your paycheck taken out and put into your savings account.

Look over your insurance plans.

Check all of your insurance policies to see what they cover. That is, you might have too much and be wasting it, or you might not have enough and not be safe. Virginia CU Insurance Services can help you find the best coverage at a price you can afford.

Being careful with purchases that happen often

It's not a good idea to spend a lot of money on things that you will use again and again, like gifts and trips. It might feel good to spend money at the time, but you might wish you had it later.

Lessen or cut back on your services.

Is it possible to get a cheaper cable package or not have any cable at all? If you have a cell phone, you might want to get rid of your landline.

Try cutting down on your energy costs.

Everything should be turned off when not in use. Buy light bulbs that use less energy. When you can, use a fan instead of the air conditioner or a sweater instead of the heater.

Sign up for an online service that lets you pay your bills.

You'll save money on stamps and make sure your payments get to the right people on time. Members of VACU can use the online Bill Pay service for free.

Eat out less often and order takeout.

The cost of the lunch might add up if you ate it every day, no matter how little it was. In a year, a $10 pizza once a week will cost you more than $500.

How to Spend Money Wisely

This means getting the most for your money when it comes to what's important to you. This makes you want to save even more, which helps you stay on track to reach your financial goals.

Being smart about spending means living a simple life and finding smart ways to save money. If you change a few habits and set some financial goals, you may become a smart spender.

You might find it helpful to divide your spending into four groups: Needs, Wants, Savings, and Paying Down Debt.

Needs

These are the costs you can't avoid that help you feed, house, and keep your family safe. Some of these are your mortgage or rent, food shopping, utilities, transportation, and the minimum payments on your loans and other debts. In case your employer has already taken them out of your pay, don't forget to add any taxes you owe.

Wants

These are all the things you buy that you don't need. Some of them are going out to eat, seeing a movie, shopping for new clothes, joining a gym, taking a vacation, and buying concert tickets.

Money saved or debts paid off.

You can use the money you save in many ways, like when you're trying to get back on your feet after a financial disaster, when you need to take a much-needed vacation, or when you finally reach a long-term goal (such as retirement). As long as you make at least the minimum payment on your debts every month, they are considered debts. When making choices about what to buy, it's smart to keep these three things in mind. If you notice that you are spending too much in one area, it could mean that you need to change the way you spend your money.

Ways to Make a Plan to Spend Money

It's great to make money as a teen. Although it's freeing, having a lot of power comes with a lot of responsibility. These tips will help you spend your money wisely so that you don't start as an adult broke. Here are some tips to help you deal with your money:

1. Create a Budget

To get a true picture of your finances, keep track of how much you earn and how much you spend. You can keep your receipts or write down what you buy as you go. Go over your bills and add them to your budget every month.

- Put your purchases in order by type (food, clothing, entertainment, etc.). The categories that spend the most money each month (or the ones that spend shockingly much each month) might be the best places to start saving money.

- Once you've been keeping track of your purchases for a while, set a monthly (or weekly) limit for each category. Make sure that your total budget is less than the money you make during that time, and if you can, leave some extra money for savings.

2. Plan Your Purchases In Advance

If you make snap decisions, your costs could go through the roof. While you're at home, taking it easy, write down what you need to buy.

- Take a trip to get ready for your main shopping trip. Write down the prices of a few different options at one or more stores.

- Every purchase should be seen as an important choice. This will help you make better decisions.

- It is not okay to take free samples or try things on for fun. Even if you're not going to buy it.

3. Avoid Impulse Purchases

It is smart to plan ahead, but it is not smart to buy something on the spur of the moment. If you want to avoid making bad buying decisions, follow these rules:

- Don't just look around or go shopping for the sake of it. If all you want to do is buy something because you enjoy shopping.

- Don't make purchase decisions if you can't trust your judgment. It's possible that alcohol, other drugs, or not getting enough sleep could make it harder for you to make good decisions.

4. Shop Alone

You might want to spend more money because of your kids, friends who like shopping, or even a friend whose tastes you admire.

5. Pay in Full and in Cash

Credit and debit cards make you spend more because they give you more money to spend than you would have otherwise and because no money is visible changing hands, the transaction is not seen as "real."

6. Don't Be Fooled By Marketing

We spend our money in big ways because of things outside of our control. Keep an eye out for all the things that make you want a product.

- Don't make a purchase based only on advertising.
- Don't buy something just because it's on sale.
- Be wary of price gimmicks.
- Don't always go for the lowest-priced item in a category.

7. Wait for sales and discounts
We spend our money in big ways because of things outside of our control. Keep an eye out for all the things that make you want a product.

8. Conduct Research
We spend our money in big ways because of things outside of our control. Keep an eye out for all the things that make you want a product.

9. Take All The Costs Into Account
A lot of big-ticket items will cost you a lot more than what they say they will. Before making a choice, read the fine print and add up all the numbers.

10. Only Purchase What You Actually Need
Check your closet to see what you already have. You can get a better idea of your condition by selling or giving away things you don't wear or that don't fit.

Understanding Budgeting and Its Importance

You will need a budget to keep track of your money and reach your financial goals. A personal or household budget shows how much money you make and how much you spend over a certain period, usually one month.

When you hear the word "budget," you might think of controlling spending. But a budget doesn't have to be efficient to work. You can see how much money you expect to get each month, as well as your necessary costs (like rent and insurance) and your extra spending (like entertainment or eating out).

Instead of seeing a budget as something that gets in the way, see it as something that will help you reach your financial goals.

What Does a Budget Do?

A monthly budget is a written plan for your money that helps you figure out how much you will spend and save each month. If you want to, you can also keep track of how much money you spend each month.

Making a budget is necessary to keep your finances in order. The reason for this is that budgets need to be balanced. When you spend less in one area, you can spend more in another, save for a big purchase, build a "rainy day" fund, save more, or help your wealth grow.

Last, your new budget will show you where your money comes from, how much you have, and how much you spend every month.

The Easy Way to Make a Budget

Before you can make a budget that helps you live a happy and comfortable life, you need to figure out how much you are spending now, how much you can afford to spend, and what your goals are. Pick out a good template to put in your income and expenses before you start making a budget.

Get your financial documents together.

Get all of your financial records together before you start. You need to be able to see everything you earn and spend. Finding the average for each month is one of the most important steps in making a budget. It is helpful to learn as much as you can.

Figure out your income.

How much money do you think you'll make each month? You can use your net income, also known as "take-home pay," if you get paid regularly and taxes are taken out automatically.

Make a list of your monthly bills.

Write down all the bills you need to pay in a month. To keep track of how much you've spent, look at your bank and credit card statements from the last three months.

Find out what your fixed and variable costs are.

There are some costs that you always have to pay the same amount for; these are called fixed costs. Mortgage or rent payments, car payments, fixed-fee internet access, trash pickup, and regular child care should all be added to the list of costs. Include any other important spending that you expect to keep up every month if you make your credit card payment on time.

If you plan to save a certain amount of money each month or pay off a certain amount of debt each month, those costs should be added as fixed expenses. Some costs that change from month to month are groceries, gas, entertainment, eating out, gifts, and so on. Check your credit card or bank bills from the last two or three months to see how much you spend in each area.

Add up your monthly income and bills.

You're on the right track if your income is higher than your costs. With this extra money, you can put it toward other parts of your budget, like saving for retirement or paying off debt. If your spending is more than your income, you're paying too much and need to make some changes.

Change how much you spend.

If your spending is higher than your income, look for places in your variable costs where you can cut back. Think about ways to save money, like eating out less or canceling a subscription-like your gym membership. If you have a lot of debt or spend more than you earn, cutting back on your variable costs might not be enough. To balance your budget, you might need to cut back on fixed costs and bring in more money.

Different Budgeting Strategies

Here's a deeper look at five fundamental budgeting principles.

1. 50/30/20 Budget

A list of needs, wants, and savings is used to figure out the 50/30/20 method. It can be hard to tell the difference between costs that you need and costs that you want, but here are some general tips on how to divide your after-tax income:

50% Needs / Non-negotiable Essentials

- Housing (mortgage/rent)
- Groceries
- Utility bills
- Loan payments at a minimum (credit cards, student loans)

30% Wants / Personal Expenses

- Dining out
- Entertainment/events
- Travel

20% Savings

- Emergency-fund savings
- Retirement savings
- Debt repayment (payments in excess of the statutory minimum)

The 50/30/20 rule strives to provide you with a well-rounded lifestyle with the proper financial balance, including basic spending, unanticipated expenses, and even items you like while saving for your future.

2. Zero-Based Budget

It might be scary to think about having no money, but zero-based budgeting (ZBB) isn't about spending all of your money. With ZBB, you take out your monthly expenses from your monthly income until you have enough left over to pay for whatever is most important that month. This process continues until you reach zero. This means that you're trying to reach a zero-waste situation where no money is lost.

You can do this by putting your spending into groups. For the most part, the main categories write themselves (food, housing, utilities, transportation). Other important categories include extra bills, paying off debt, savings, entertainment, and other fees.

3. Envelope Budget

In this old-fashioned method, you divide up real money and put it in different envelopes for each of your monthly bills. When you use a debit or credit card, the impact may be "out of sight, out of mind," but when you spend cash, you feel it in your hands every time. Because the money in each envelope has to last for the whole month and can't be replaced, being more aware of your finances can help you stay on track with your goals.

The cash envelopes will be used for costs that move around during the month, like:

- Groceries
- Utility bills that fluctuate
- Transportation
- Discretionary spending

Figure out how much you usually pay for each of these fees every month so you know how much cash you need to take out. Just put the right amount of money in each envelope and take money out as you need it.

4. Values-Based Budget
In addition to making sure you have enough money for things like food, shelter, utilities, and transportation, values-based budgeting means spending any extra money on things or causes that are important to you. One way to look at how you're spending your money now and how you'd like to spend it in the future is to look at your bank statements from the last three months and think about what you value.

For example, you might find that most of your extra money is spent on eating out after looking over your spending records. You like to try new places and go on adventures. You also like to help charities and groups in need and keep yourself healthy and fit. Here are some ways you could spend your money differently:

- Save forty percent of your extra money to go to restaurants you like or find new ones.

- Give 30% of your remaining money to local businesses, organizations, and social projects whose work you agree with (bonus points if you also offer your time to volunteer).

- Spend the last 30% of your money on a course to improve yourself or a program to improve your health.

5. Pay Yourself First Budget
The name of the budgeting method makes it sound like it goes against all the rules, but it doesn't. On the other hand, this plan only

puts your savings first. As with any budget, you start by finding out how much money you make each month. Set monthly savings goals, each with a cash amount, instead of writing down your monthly expenses or breaking down your income into categories or percentages. Then, take your monthly net income and subtract all of your savings. You could use the extra money to pay bills and other costs.

This is how a savings-oriented budget may look:

- **Monthly net income:** $3,600

- **Monthly savings goals:** retirement fund ($300), 529 plan ($250), emergency fund ($200), vacation fund ($200), landscaping backyard upgrade ($200) = $1,150

- **Spending money:** $3,600 (net income) - $1,150 (savings) = $2,450

- Use the remaining $2,450 to fulfill your monthly costs.

Emergency Funds

An emergency fund is a bank account with money set aside to pay for big, unexpected costs like

- Unforeseen medical expenses.

- Home-appliance repair or replacement.

- Major car fixes.

- Unemployment.

Importance of Emergency Fund

Emergency reserves provide a financial cushion that can keep you afloat in times of need without requiring you to rely on credit cards or high-interest loans.

Advantages of Emergency Funds

Putting together an emergency fund has these benefits:

1. Lowers levels of stress

In an emergency, like losing your job suddenly, having trouble with your car, or needing to fix things around the house, these things can put your financial health at risk, which can cause stress.

2. Makes people more likely to save

People are more likely to save money and less likely to spend it on unnecessary things like TVs and game systems when they have an emergency fund.

3. Keeps bad debt from happening

If people had an emergency fund, they wouldn't have to think about using bad debt, like high-interest credit cards, to pay for things they need. If you use this kind of debt, you might have to pay more because of extra interest, fees, and penalties for being careless.

Sinking Funds

One type of fund that was created and set up specifically to pay off debt is a sinking fund. The person who has the account regularly sets aside a set amount of money and only uses it for one thing. It's usually used by corporations to deposit money and buy back bonds or parts of bonds before they mature. Additionally, it is a way to get investors because the fund helps them believe that the issuer will keep its promises.

Why sinking funds are important

Many people know what a sinking fund is because even kids in school know that it's an important and useful way to save money for something they want to buy or have. In school, if a class wants to end the year with a field trip to the zoo, they can start a sinking fund. By the end of the year, it will have grown to the right amount and can be used to pay for the trip. The students don't have to use their own money because they've been putting money into their sinking fund all year. To sum up, a sinking fund is proactive because it helps a person plan for future expenses.

Advantages of Sinking Funds

Here are some of the good things about sinking funds:

1. Brings in money from investors

Most investors are aware that companies or groups that have a lot of debt could be risky.

2. The chance that interest rates will go down

A company with bad credit will have a hard time getting investors unless it offers higher interest rates.

3. Stable Money

A company's financial situation isn't always stable, and some money worries could shake up its strong base.

First Thing You Should Do with Every Paycheck

You can finally buy that TV you've been eyeing for a few weeks now that you've finally earned some money. We understand that you want to spend all of your money, but wait! There are some things you need to do first.

1. Put money into your 401k

Start putting away your salary for retirement if you want to have the best retirement ever. Experts in money say that putting money into your 401k account when you get paid is a good idea.

2. Save some money.

Aside from putting money into a retirement account, you should also save some of your money.

3. Pay off your debts

They need to pay off their debts first. It is best to pay it all off if you can. If you don't, pay off your credit card debt and other debts with high interest rates first. You might save money in the long run if you pay off your debts with the highest interest rates first. But you should also remember to pay off any bills that are past due. If you owe a lot of money and bill collectors are calling you, you should pay it off as soon as possible. You can do this by consolidating your debt or paying off your higher-interest debts first.

4. Make a budget for your money

Another thing that experts agree on is that you should plan how you'll spend your money before you do it. Plan how you will spend your hard-earned money. But having a budget isn't so bad. The majority of people find that making a budget gives them the freedom and permission to spend.

5. Keep track of every dollar

When you keep track of every dollar, you can plan your paychecks better. When you're making your budget, write down how much money you make and how much you spend. Name each dollar.

There's something you should do with your pay before you even get it. Before giving you a dollar, it has to be accounted for, even if it's because you spent too much, which is fine.

6. Spend money on yourself

Investing in yourself is the most important thing you'll ever do. You've probably heard this before, but it's true. This doesn't mean you have to spend a lot of money on yourself, though. Instead, it means putting money into yourself "through learning, mentoring, and personal growth."

Automate Your Finances

Always keeping your long-term goals in mind takes a lot of work and self-control. However, it is easier to reach your goals if you have a plan in place that replaces willpower and gets rid of temptation.

You can reach your financial goals by consciously creating good long-term habits and resisting the urge to stray from your plan when you automate your money.

Steps to Automating Your Finances

Sign up for online bill payment and set up automatic payments.

Most people think that you can only set up automatic credit card payments. But did you know that you can do this for any regular cost, like your rent, cell phone bill, utility bills, or even your car insurance? But remember that setting up automatic payments does not mean you don't have to check your bills and account statements. Check all of those things twice before they are taken out of your checking account to avoid overdrafts or fraudulent payments.

Put money away automatically for the future.

A key part of getting out of the rat race is paying yourself. You should save some of your pay every month for retirement.

If you have a 401k through your job, this could happen before you even get paid. If your company doesn't offer a 401k, you should look into IRAs and set up a way to make monthly payments to one.

Setting up a regular deposit to your savings account will do it for you.

Building up an emergency fund should always be your first goal when you start saving. You should save enough money to cover your living costs for three to six months. It's best not to touch it unless it's something really important. Don't forget to make this process automatic as well.

Savings will add up without you having to think about it.

Budgeting tools can help you keep track of the money you spend.

Keeping track of your spending and making budgets are important, but they can take a lot of time. If you want to set financial goals, free budgeting software can help you figure out how much you need to save and how much you can spend each month.

Useful tools for Managing your Finances
Divvy.com
Divvy is a billing company and business expenditure management system that consists of two major components: 1) real and virtual charge cards and 2) expense and management software that records spending from those charge cards. This article will provide you with an introduction to how Divvy operates and some of the features you will have access to as a Divvy customer.

How Divvy Works

If a business wants to work with Divvy, they have to fill out an application with some basic information about their business.

It depends on the outcome of this application to decide whether the company can get an unsecured line of credit or not. If approved, the business will be given a credit line that tells them how much they can spend on Divvy cards.

Charge Card

Charge cards are used to pay for things on Divvy. Charge cards can be used for business transactions just like any other card, as long as the budget that is linked to the card has enough money in it. When the month is over, you have to pay the full amount on your charge card.

Physical Cards

Administrators can give real charge cards to each user when they are added to Divvy so that they can use them for business costs. Users can also be given budgets that tell them how much money they can spend. With the Divvy mobile app, users can quickly activate their charge cards.

Virtual Cards

Along with real cards, administrators and spenders can make as many virtual cards as they need in their Divvy account. All virtual cards are different and come with their own security code and card number. They are great for online and recurring purchases.

Expense & Spend Management Software

All Divvy users can get to the platform through a web browser or the Divvy mobile app. Divvy administrators may simply examine and manage transactions from all charge cards in their business, remit cash to spenders, and adjust account settings. Spenders have the ability to see and classify their transactions, request cash, and create virtual cards.

You can read more about some of Divvy's software features below.

- **Budgets:** Budgets let Divvy account managers control how the charge cards in their accounts are used. Customers can keep track of all of their spending under one budget or make multiple budgets to get a better handle on the different types of spending their business makes.
- **Insights:** The Insights page lets Divvy administrators compare how much money was spent in their account during a certain time period to a previous time period. You can change these insights so that they only show spending amounts for certain budgets, merchants, spenders, and custom fields.
- **Integrations:** QuickBooks Online, QuickBooks Desktop, NetSuite, and Sage Intacct are the accounting programs that Divvy works with.
- **People:** QuickBooks Online, QuickBooks Desktop, NetSuite, and Sage Intacct are the accounting programs that Divvy works with.
- **Reimbursements:** Reimbursements can be used to add business transactions that don't use a Divvy charge card to the Divvy platform. People who spend money may get reimbursed for things like mileage and out-of-pocket costs. Using the Divvy platform, admins can say no to or yes to these requests.
- **Transactions:** On the Divvy platform, you can look at transactions that matter to you right now, whether you are an administrator or a spender. You can finish up recent transactions by filling out the right fields and uploading receipts from a web browser or the app. Admins can decide which transactions need

to be approved based on the amount and/or budget limits. They can easily review these transactions on their phone or laptop.

Mint Budgeting App

Mint is one of the most popular tools for making budgets these days. Mint began in 2006 and was bought by the software company Intuit in 2009. You can read our review of the Mint app to learn more about it, such as its features, price, and reviews, and then decide if it's right for you.

With over 924,737 reviews on the App Store and Google Play, Mint gets better ratings from users than its competitors. Forbes Advisors named Mint one of the Best Budgeting Apps, so you should think about using it to help you with your budgeting needs.

An app for your phone called Mint can help you make a budget automatically and find ways to save money for future goals. As of March 4, 2022, the account information and fees are correct.

Distinguishing Features

Mint account holders can get their credit scores and use tools to keep an eye on their credit for free. You can get to your TransUnion VantageScore whenever you want, thanks to a partnership with TransUnion. Checking your credit score with Mint won't hurt your credit score in any way.

Your credit score is a snapshot of your credit history, along with information about how scores are calculated and what you can do to raise your score. TransUnion also lets Mint offer free credit monitoring. TransUnion lets users sign up to be notified right away whenever the company gets new information from creditors.

Chapter 06: Paying Off Student Loans

How Budgeting After College Can Help Repay Student Loans

It's almost impossible to get ahead financially without first learning how to make a budget. College is a great time to start keeping track of your money. Making a budget is a two-step process that shows how well you can handle your money.

The first thing you need to do is add up all of your monthly income from all sources. That could be money from a job, your parents, or the college's financial aid office (loans, scholarships, or grants). After college, that list usually gets shorter to just your job and any help your parents can give you.

The second step is to write down all of your costs, which could take some time. Some examples of fixed costs are rent, utilities, food, phone/cable bills, and maybe a car loan.

Take your total income and subtract your fixed costs to get your disposable income. This is the money you can spend on things like going out to eat, the movies, sports games, transportation, laundry, clothes, and medical care.

When students graduate with a lot of debt, they often have no idea what happened to all of their extra cash. The same is true after graduation. A budget that breaks down your spending into every possible category will show you that you spend money in places you didn't expect.

Here are some ideas on how to lighten the spending of disposable income:

- **Live Like A College Kid:** Some college traditions are worth preserving, at least temporarily. To split rent and costs, you can keep roommates. Nothing helps a budget more than paying half or a third of rent and utilities for one person.

- **Smart Clothing:** Dressier clothes are needed in the workplace, but there are smart ways to construct a professional wardrobe. Buy high-quality, adaptable business apparel. In everyday situations, dress down (at least for now).

- **Learn to Cook:** Dining out wrecks budgets. When out, drinking adds to the problem. Start with simple recipes and cook at home. You should drink water wherever you eat. Includes a glass of water.

- **Don't Drive Alone:** That means carpooling. It could also mean public transit. In the right city, it may mean walking without a car. No gas, insurance, repairs, or vehicle payment = financial independence.

Ways to Make A Plan To Pay Off Student Loans

As you know, debt is unavoidable. You need discipline. It requires sacrifice. It needs... strategy. Always record goals. It gives them depth and vitality. It motivates, too.

Here are some steps to follow.

- **Use The Grace Period:** It takes between six months and a year after graduation for lenders to let you off the hook on your loan. Why not start right away? If your payment is $300 a month after the grace period, you need to get ahead of the debt right away.

You will also get into the habit of putting $300 away every month.

- **Research Your Loans:** Don't just turn off your brain and let the minimum payment happen on its own. On the National Student Loan Data System, you can find all of your federal loan repayment plans. Your credit report, which lists the names of your lenders, might be given to you for free. Depending on how much money you make, you could choose an income-based repayment plan. You might want to look into debt consolidation. Check to see if you can receive a loan forgiveness, a deferment, or a better payment plan for your debts.

- **Increase Your Income:** At your first job, you probably won't get a raise, but you might be able to work extra hours. You could also get a second job or do something extra on the side. You might be able to sell your skills or services. All of these things could bring in money to pay off debt.

- **Deduct:** If you paid interest on student loans during the tax year, you might be able to get up to $2,500 off of your taxable income. It doesn't matter how little.

- **Seek Loan Forgiveness:** As a benefit, some employers pay off student loans. In some jobs, like those in the government or with 501(c)(3) nonprofits, you may be able to get your debt forgiven after ten years of payments. You can also get your loans forgiven if you work in a low-income area or a rural town that doesn't have enough teachers, doctors, lawyers, dentists, social workers, or other in-demand professionals.

- **Sign Up For Auto-Debit:** If you set up an automatic payment plan with some lenders, they may lower your interest rate. This plan will also keep you from getting fined for being late or missing payments.

- **Avoid More Big Debts:** It may seem obvious that you shouldn't use your credit card to buy something big or get another loan, but not everyone is smart. If you have plans for a big wedding, a fancy car, or a house, you might need to change them soon.

How To Avoid Defaulting On Student Loans

You can be sure that your student loan payments will not just disappear if you can't make the minimum monthly payments.

- You haven't paid in 90 days, so you're late. If you don't pay it in 270 days (nine months), you've turned down the debt, and you could face serious consequences.
- You have as much time as you need to pay off your student loans. It's almost impossible to get rid of them by filing for bankruptcy. They'll stick with you your whole life. You shouldn't think you can get away.
- Some federal student loans have 6% late payment fees that you may have to pay extra if you are late. And finally, the government can take up to 15% of your paycheck and Social Security payments. The government may also take 25% of each payment to cover collection costs, which will make the loan more expensive.
- Payments you miss or are late on will hurt your credit score and stay on your record for up to seven years.
- About $138 billion in student loan debt is past due. Two out of every five people who have student loans are behind on their payments in the first five years.
- Ask for a delay or forbearance if you can't make payments. Your credit score will not go down if you use either method. When your account is brought up to date, your score will go up.
- If you lose your job or get sick for a short time, you can temporarily stop making payments on your federal student loans. The downside is that you will keep paying interest on your debts, which will make them more expensive in the long run.
- For federal student loans, you can also choose from a number of different payment plans, such as Income-Based Repayment, Pay

As You Earn, Revised Pay As You Earn, and Income-Based Repayment.
- Contingent Plan, which would lower monthly payments and make the debt last longer. With these plans, your payment is based on how much money you make, and you won't be late payment as long as you pay on time every month.
- Getting a free credit report once a year is a good idea to make sure that it accurately shows your payment history.
- Nothing at all should lead to default! It is better to talk to your loan servicer about your options for paying back the loan if you can't make the payment than to just not pay. If you get help as soon as possible, you can come up with a plan that works for you and your budget.

Tips For Managing Your Student Loan Debt

About 43 million Americans have student loan debt right now. 1 If you're trying to get or stay financially stable, you know how hard it can be to keep up with all of your obligations at the same time. You may have options if you want to find a lower interest rate, lower your monthly payment, or even pay off some of your student loans and be done with them. These seven ideas might help you get started on paying off your student loans and feel better about it while you still enjoy your life. Here are some tips that will help you pay off your school debt:

1. Don't forget about them

Don't rely on used loan information either, and don't just skim the news. This is a simple but important point. If you don't pay your student loans, it could hurt your credit score and cost you money in fines and fees that could hurt your finances in the long run.

2. Take a look at your loans.

Private or public lenders can give out student loans, and the interest rate on each loan may change based on when you applied for it. The National Student Loan Data System has a list of your federal loans, how much you owe, and how much you pay each month. You could also add your personal loans to this list to get a good idea of how much money you need to save each month for your budget.

3. Look for special shows

As talks about federal forgiveness continue, keep your eyes and ears open. There may be government or non-profit organizations that forgive student loans. Non-profit hospitals and schools are two examples. Make sure you understand the rules well so you can decide if you are eligible to participate. Some companies may also offer benefits related to getting rid of student debt.

4. Look over your options for refinancing and consolidating

Putting all of your student loans into one loan with one monthly payment may help if you have a lot of them. Otherwise, if you have a loan with a high interest rate, you could try to refinance it with a lower rate.

When you consolidate or refinance your debt, make sure you know:

- ✓ Your new interest rate
- ✓ Any cost to consolidate or refinance
- ✓ if the new interest can change at a future time
- ✓ To find out whether you may pay back your loan in full or if there are any prepayment restrictions,

You might pay more interest over time if you pay off the loan over ten years instead of 5. This is true even if the interest rate is lower.

5. Find a way to pay that works for you.

Those who have federal student loans may be able to choose a payment plan that costs less. You can choose to extend the length of your loan beyond the usual ten years. For some, you can make smaller monthly payments at first and larger ones later on. This might help your budget if you're just starting in the job market.

Figure out the plan that will help your cash flow the most now and in the future. If you want to get your debt forgiven, make sure you pick one of the program's options for income-based repayment.

6. If you're having a hard time, think about your specific situation.

If you are having trouble with money, like when you lose your job, you might be able to get a deferment, which means you can stop making payments for a while. Interest usually doesn't build up during deferral. Forbearance is another option. It's the same as deferral, but you will usually still have to pay interest on your loan.

7. Don't put student loans ahead of everything else.

Even if you have a lot of student loans to pay off, make sure you're also spending your money wisely in other areas. First, you should make sure that you pay at least the minimum amount on all of your student loans. You're on your own after that. You might feel better about putting more money into your employer's retirement plan so that you don't lose money. And if you want to pay off credit card debt, you should know that it has a higher interest rate than student debt. This means that it costs more to borrow money with a credit card.

Chapter 07: Investing for Increasing Your Assets

Understanding Investing

Investing means putting money or other resources into something with the goal of making a profit. When you invest, you can put your money into businesses or assets. For example, you might buy real estate with the goal of selling it later for a higher price. Investing is based on the idea that you will get a return, either in the form of income or a rise in the value of your investments. You can invest in a lot of different things and get a return on your money.

When it comes to investments, risk and return go hand in hand. Low risk usually means low expected profits, while higher returns usually mean higher risk. CDs and other basic investments are thought to be low-risk. Bonds and other fixed-income instruments are thought to be higher risk, while stocks and other equities are thought to be higher risk. A lot of people think that commodities and derivatives are some of the riskiest investments you can make. You can also put your money into something useful, like land or real estate, or something fragile, like fine art and antiques.

Expectations for risk and return can be very different, even within the same asset class. A micro-cap that trades on a small exchange will have a very different risk-return profile than a blue chip that trades on the New York Stock Exchange. The type of asset determines the returns it brings in. Many stocks, for instance, pay dividends every three months, but bonds usually pay interest every three months. In many countries, different types of income are taxed at different rates.

One important part of the return is price growth, along with regular income like dividends or interest. So, the total return on investment can be thought of as the sum of the interest earned and the value of the investment going up. Standard & Poor's says that since 1926, capital gains have made up two-thirds of total equity return, and dividends have made up about a third.

Types of Investments

There are a lot of different kinds of investments, but these are the most common ones:

Stocks

When someone buys stock in a company, they become a part-owner of that company. Shareholders own a company's stock and can have a say in how it grows and succeeds by seeing the stock price rise and receiving monthly dividends from the company's profits. Bonds are debt obligations that are issued by groups like businesses, governments, and cities. When you buy a bond, you become a part owner of a company's debt. You will receive interest payments over time and the face value of the bond when it matures.

Funds

Funds are pooled products that are managed by investment managers and used to invest in stocks, bonds, commodities, and other assets. Mutual funds, exchange-traded funds, and closed-end funds are all types of funds. Most of the time, people use mutual funds and exchange-traded funds, or ETFs. Mutual funds don't trade on an exchange, so their value is set at the end of the trading day. ETFs, on the other hand, trade on stock exchanges, so their value changes all day, just like stocks. One way that mutual funds and ETFs can follow benchmarks is passively, like the S&P 500. Another way is active, like the Dow Jones Industrial Average.

Trusts for investments

Another type of pooled investment is a trust. The most common type is a real estate investment trust (REIT). REITs buy commercial or residential properties and give their investors monthly dividends based on how much rent these properties bring in. REITs trade on stock markets, which gives investors quick access to their money.

Other ways to invest

This is a general term for private equity and hedge funds. Hedge funds get their name from the fact that they can place bets on stocks and other investments, both long and short. With private equity, a company can get money without going public. In the past, hedge funds and private equity were only open to "accredited investors" who were wealthy enough to meet strict income and net worth requirements. Alternative investments, on the other hand, are now available in fund forms that regular investors can use.

Different kinds of options

Derivatives are types of financial instruments whose value is based on the value of another instrument, like an index or stock. An option is a common derivative that gives the buyer the right but not the duty to buy or sell a security at a set price within a certain amount of time. Most derivatives are borrowed, which makes them high-risk, high-reward investments.

Commodities

Metals, oil, grain, and animal products are all examples of commodities. Money and financial instruments are also examples of commodities. You can trade them with commodity futures, which are contracts to buy or sell a certain amount of a commodity at a set price on a certain date in the future, or exchange-traded funds (ETFs). You can use commodities to hedge your risk or just for fun.

Learning How the Stock Market Works

A Stock

Stocks are a type of money that gives investors a claim on a company's assets (what it owns) and earnings (what it generates in profits). Some other names for stocks are shares and a company's equity. When a person owns stock, they own a piece of the company equal to the number of shares they own as a percentage of all the shares that are out there. For instance, someone or something that owns 100,000 shares of a company that has a million shares out there has a 10% interest in that company. Most of the time, millions or even billions of shares in a company are being bought and sold.

Different Kinds of Stock

There are two kinds of stock: common and preferred. When we talk about "equities," we're really talking about common shares because their market value and trading volume are so much higher than those of preferred shares. The main difference between the two is that common shares usually come with voting rights, which let the owner have a say in corporate meetings (like the annual general meeting or AGM), where things like choosing auditors and electing new board members are decided. Preferred shares, on the other hand, do not come with voting rights. Preferred shares get dividends and assets before common shareholders in the event of a liquidation. This is how the name "preferred" came about.

There are a lot of different ways to group the voting rights of common stock. The basic idea behind common stock is that each share should have the same voting rights. However, some companies have two or more classes of stock, and each has different voting rights.

In a two-class structure, Class A shares might have ten votes each, while Class B subordinate voting shares might only have one vote each. Dual- or multiple-class share arrangements are meant to give the founders of a company control over its finances, strategic direction, and ability to come up with new ideas.

Why do businesses give out shares?

The huge company we know today was probably started as a small private company by an ambitious businessman many years ago. For example, Jack Ma started Alibaba (BABA) from his home in Hangzhou, China, in 1999. Mark Zuckerberg started the first version of Facebook (now Meta) from his dorm room at Harvard University in 2004. In just a few decades, tech giants like these have become some of the most powerful companies in the world.

But in order to grow so quickly, they need access to a huge amount of capital. An entrepreneur needs to rent an office or factory, hire workers, buy tools and materials, and set up a sales and distribution network in order to turn an idea into a business. Based on how big and broad the company is at first, these resources will cost a lot of money.

Getting More Money

A new business can get these funds by either borrowing money or selling shares (equity financing) (debt financing). Debt financing can be hard for a startup because it might not have many assets to put up as collateral for a loan. This is especially true in technology or biotechnology, where companies don't have many physical assets. Also, the interest on the loan would be expensive in the beginning, when the company might not be making any money. With this in mind, equity financing is the best option for almost all businesses that need money. The business owner might use their own money as well as money from friends and family to get the business off the ground. Entrepreneurs may turn to angel investors and venture capital firms as their business grows and needs more money.

Putting up shares

When starting a business, it may need access to much larger amounts of money than it can get from regular work or a traditional bank loan. It can do this by holding an IPO and selling shares to everyone (the public) (IPO).

This changes the company from a private corporation, where only a few shareholders own shares, to a publicly traded company, where many people besides the shareholders will own shares.

The initial public offering (IPO) also lets early investors in the company cash out a portion of their stake, which usually leads to very high returns. When a company's shares are put on a stock market and trading starts, the price of those shares changes as investors and traders decide how much they are worth.

The most well-known ratio and indicator that can be used to look at companies is the price-to-earnings (PE) ratio. You can look at stocks in two different ways: fundamentally and technically.

Stock Exchange Market

Stock exchanges are like secondary markets where current shareholders can buy and sell shares with people who want to buy shares. It is important to know that companies that are traded on stock markets don't usually buy and sell their own shares. Companies can buy back their own shares or issue more shares, but these aren't normal business activities and often happen outside of an exchange's control.

That is, when you buy stock on the stock exchange, you don't buy it from the company itself but from another shareholder. Also, when you sell your shares, you don't sell them back to the company; you sell them to another investor.

Stock Market Example

Name	Region	Market Capitalization
New York Stock Exchange	United States	$25.6 trillion
NASDAQ	United States	$19.5 trillion
Shanghai Stock Exchange	China	$6.9 trillion
Euronext Stock Exchange	Netherlands	$6.8 trillion
Hong Kong Stock Exchange	Hong Kong	$6.1 trillion
Tokyo Stock Exchange	Japan	$5.6 trillion
Shenzhen Stock Exchange	China	$5 trillion
London Stock Exchange	England	$4.3 trillion
Toronto Stock Exchange	Canada	$2.9 trillion
Bombay Stock Exchange	India	$2.8 trillion

Functions of a Stock Market

These are the main things that a stock exchange does:

Openness in the Trading of Securities

The stock exchange has to make sure that everyone who wants to see information about all buy and sell orders can get it at the right time. This helps make sure that prices for securities are fair and clear, based on rules about supply and demand. Also, it should match related buy and sell orders quickly and correctly. Three people may have put in orders to buy Microsoft shares at $100, $105, and $110, and four people may be ready to sell Microsoft shares for $110, $112, $115, and $120. The exchange has to make sure that the best buy and best sell prices are equal, which, in this case, is $110 for the given trade amount. This is done by automated trading systems.

That Works for Price Discovery

Price discovery in the stock market is the process of figuring out the right price for an asset. This is usually done by looking at supply and demand in the market, as well as other factors of the transactions.

Let's say that a software company in the US has a market value of $5 billion and a price per share of $100. Reports say that the European Union (EU) authority has fined the company $2 billion, which means that 40% of the company's value may be lost. The stock market may have set a trading price range for the company's shares between $90 and $110. However, it should effectively adjust the trading price limit to account for expected changes in the share price. If it doesn't, shareholders may have trouble trading at a fair price.

Keeping the cash flow steady

The stock market needs to make sure that everyone qualified and ready to trade can immediately place orders that will be filled at a fair price, even if there are too many buyers and sellers of a certain financial instrument.

Safety and reliability of transactions

Even though more players are necessary for a market to work well, that market must make sure that all of its participants are checked out and continue to follow the rules, leaving no room for either party to default. It should also make sure that all businesses in the market that are connected to it follow the rules and act in a way that is allowed by the rules.

Help all market participants who are qualified.

People who take part in a marketplace are market makers, investors, traders, speculators, and hedgers. Each of these groups does different things in the stock market. Investors might buy stocks and hold on to them for a few years, but traders can enter and leave a position in a matter of seconds. A market maker is very important for keeping the market liquid, while a hedger might choose to trade in derivatives to lower the risk of their investments. The stock market should make sure that all of these players can easily do their jobs so that the market can continue to work efficiently.

Defense for Investors

Rich people and large businesses aren't the only ones who invest in the stock market. A lot of small investors also use it to make small investments. These investors might not know much about money and the risks that come with buying stocks and other publicly traded instruments. For investors to keep their money and for customers to trust the stock exchange, the right safety measures must be put in place. For example, a stock exchange might divide stocks into different groups based on how risky they are and let regular investors trade in high-risk stocks less or not at all. Exchanges usually put limits on people who want to trade risky derivatives so that people with little money and knowledge don't do it.

Regulation That Is Fair

Listed companies are subject to a lot of rules, and market regulators like the SEC keep an eye on their transactions. To make sure that everyone in the market is aware of what's going on, exchanges also have rules like making sure that quarterly financial reports are turned in on time and that any important events are reported right away. If you don't follow the rules, the exchanges may suspend your trade and take other disciplinary actions.

Individual Retirement Account (IRA) vs Non-Retirement Brokerage Accounts

Individual Retirement Account (IRA)

Individual Retirement Accounts (IRAs) offer a secure and tax-advantaged way to save and invest for the long term. These accounts are designed to provide individuals with a reliable and beneficial tool for their retirement planning.

Much like a 401(k)-plan offered by a company, an IRA is meant to encourage people to save for retirement. Anyone with a way to make money can open an IRA and benefit from the tax breaks that these accounts offer.

Learn about IRAs

Anyone who makes money, even people who have a 401(k) plan through their job, can open an IRA and put money into it. Only the maximum amount you can put into your retirement accounts in a single year is limited, but you will still get tax breaks.

You can put your money into a wide range of financial assets when you open an IRA, including stocks, bonds, exchange-traded funds (ETFs), and mutual funds. Other types of IRAs are self-directed IRAs (SDIRAs), which give investors more choices and let them invest in more things, like real estate and commodities. Only the riskiest investments are not allowed.

There are different kinds of IRAs, such as traditional IRAs, Roth IRAs, SEP IRAs, and SIMPLE IRAs. Each one has its own rules about who can join, pay taxes, and take money out. Standard and Roth IRAs can be opened by individuals who file taxes. SEP and SIMPLE IRAs can be opened by small business owners and people who work for themselves. You can only open an IRA at a bank that has been approved by the Internal Revenue Service (IRS) to offer these accounts. You can go to banks, brokerage firms, federally insured credit unions, or savings and loan organizations.

IRAs are meant to be used to save for retirement, so if you take money out before age 59 1⁄2, you usually have to pay a 10% penalty. There are a few important exceptions, such as withdrawals for things like buying a first home or paying for school. It will be taxed as income if you take money out of a regular IRA account instead of a Roth account.

Non-Retirement Brokerage Accounts

Brokerage accounts, unlike traditional retirement accounts, offer a high level of accessibility and flexibility. They allow you to buy and sell a variety of financial assets, including stocks, bonds, mutual funds, and exchange-traded funds (ETFs), giving you full control over your investments.

Like a bank account, you can put money in and take it out of your brokerage account. However, unlike banks, brokerage accounts give you access to the stock market and other assets.

A brokerage account is often called a "taxable account" because the money that comes in from investments is taxed as capital gains. IRAs and other retirement accounts, on the other hand, have different tax and withdrawal rules and may be better for saving and investing for retirement. A lot of people think that brokerage accounts are "not tax-favored," but there are tax benefits.

She said in an email, "The brokerage account has the benefit of leveraging the long-term capital gains tax." You have to be an investor for the long term to do that. In other words, you need to keep your assets for at least a year. Along with letting you take advantage of the best tax rate; this will almost certainly lead to higher returns. "

The rate of long-term capital gains tax changes based on your taxable income and how you file your taxes. You can choose between 0%, 15%, or 20%. Barros says that the best way to get the most out of a brokerage account is to keep the money in it, ignore the daily noise in the stock market, and "go live your life."

How Brokerage Accounts Work

You can quickly and easily open a brokerage account online with many brokers, and you don't even need a lot of money to do it. In fact, many brokerage firms let you open an account with no initial investment. You must first fund the account, though, before you can buy assets. You can move money from a checking or savings account, as well as from another brokerage account to this one. The money and investments in your brokerage account are yours, and you can sell them whenever you want. Their job is to handle your account and connect you with the investments you want to buy.

In a taxable brokerage account, you can put as much money as you want in it every year. They are both unlimited. There shouldn't be any fees for having a brokerage account.

Brokerage Account vs. IRA

Investors can have both a brokerage account and an IRA; they don't have to pick one over the other. Each account has a different purpose, uses a different method, and leads to a different set of results. A brokerage account and an individual retirement account (IRA) may help you save for retirement and buy big things like a house or car. Yu says that in both cases, you are helping to put your money to work for you by having the chance to earn a return on your assets and not falling behind on inflation.

No matter what kind of investment account you have, we always say to invest often, think long-term, and keep a broad portfolio. These three tips can help you lower your risk and put yourself in a better position to reach your own financial goals.

Because both taxable brokerage accounts and tax-deferred IRA retirement accounts have pros and cons, Anderson says investors should think about combining them. Thanks to tax breaks, IRAs may be a better way to save for retirement than brokerage accounts.

Dunn says, "A taxable brokerage account won't give you the tax deferral or even the tax advantages that an IRA does." Experts say that you should open an IRA first and then put money into a taxable brokerage account. If you want to put more money into an investment than an IRA lets you, you might want to open a brokerage account. It's more likely to grow over time if more money is put into it. If you keep doing these things, you might have more money to live on when you retire.

Index Fund

A mutual fund or exchange-traded fund (ETF) with a portfolio that is meant to copy or follow the parts of a financial market index, like the S&P 500 Index, is called an index fund (S&P 500). Index mutual funds are supposed to give investors access to a lot of different markets while also having low costs and a low turnover rate. These funds always follow their benchmark index, no matter what the market is doing.

A lot of people think that index funds are good investments for retirement accounts like 401(k) plans and individual retirement accounts (IRAs). The well-known businessman Warren Buffett says that index funds are a good place to put your retirement money. Instead of picking individual stocks to invest in, he thinks the average person would do better to buy an index fund that includes all 500 companies in the S&P 500.

The Way an Index Fund Works

The process of managing a fund without doing anything is called "indexing." A fund portfolio manager doesn't actively pick stocks or time the market, which means choosing which securities to invest in and planning when to buy and sell them. Instead, they build a portfolio whose holdings are similar to the stocks of a certain index. The idea is that if the fund matches the profile of the index, which could be the whole stock market or a large part of it, its performance will be the same as the index.

For almost every market, there is an index and an index fund. Many people in the US choose index funds that follow the S&P 500. However, a number of other indexes are often used, such as:

- ✓ The Wilshire 5000 Total Market Index is America's largest equities index.
- ✓ Stocks from Europe, Australia, and Asia are included in the MSCI EAFE Index.
- ✓ Bloomberg U.S. The Aggregate Bond Index follows the whole bond market.
- ✓ The Nasdaq Composite Index is made up of 3,000 equities that are traded on the Nasdaq market.
- ✓ The Dow Jones Industrial Average (DJIA) is a stock market index comprised of 30 large-cap corporations.

Let's say an index fund invests in the DJIA. It would buy shares in the 30 largest publicly traded companies that make up the index. The only time index fund portfolios change a lot is when their benchmark indices change. For example, if the fund is following a weighted index, the amount of different securities may change often to reflect how important they are to the benchmark. One way to balance the effect of each position in an index or portfolio is to use weighting.

Target-Date vs. Index Funds

There are two kinds of mutual funds: funds that are actively managed and funds that are passively managed (index funds). Check out Passive vs. Active Management for more information. Actively managed funds are run by portfolio managers who buy and sell assets within the fund to meet the investment goal of the fund. A type of actively managed fund called a target-date fund is meant to "mature" at a certain time.

Passively managed index funds don't change the balance of their portfolios; instead, they buy and hold a group of assets that meet the fund's goals. Both target-date funds and index funds are meant to work on their own, but to find out which is better, you need to look at a lot of different factors.

Funds that track an index

Index funds are the most basic type of mutual fund you can buy right now. These funds just buy all the stocks and bonds that are in a certain index. One example is an S&P 500 Index fund, which owns all 500 stocks in the index. Each share of the fund is equal to one voting right in all 500 companies. A fund that tracks almost every global and local financial index is called an index fund.

Planned Date Funds

Target-date funds, also known as planned-date funds, are a type of mutual fund that automatically adjusts the asset mix (stocks, bonds, and cash equivalents) over time. As the target date approaches, the fund becomes more conservative, reducing the risk of potential losses. For instance, a thrift savings plan, like the retirement plan the federal government gives to its workers, has five core funds that range from conservative to aggressive.

It also has several life cycle funds that mature every 10 years; the next one will mature in 2020. The life cycle funds hold money from the five core funds. They are funds of funds. When they are first released, the two bond funds hold 24% of the assets. The other 33% is split between the three stock funds and the five core funds. After that, the money is slowly moved around every 90 days until the goal date is reached. Second, the initial distribution is turned around. Now, 24% of the money is given to the three stock funds, and 76% is given to the two bond funds.

TD vs. Index

Comparing target-date funds and index funds can be challenging as they are structured to achieve different goals. Target-date funds, often complex organizations, aim to diversify and manage risk as the target date approaches. In contrast, index funds are straightforward, remaining unchanged over time. Index funds typically do not charge management fees, instilling confidence in their simplicity and cost-effectiveness. Target date funds can also buy different kinds of securities, like common and preferred stocks, corporate and Treasury bonds, and sometimes even other mutual funds. Also, any comparison to an index fund is automatically biased because the second type of fund is usually set up to give more conservative returns over time.

If investors want to see how these two types of funds compare, they will probably have to pick two specific funds and look at how they did over a few different but identical periods. When looking at this data, investors should keep their goals in mind, though, because people who need to access their money at a certain time, like when the target date comes up, might not be good candidates for an index fund because the index could drop a lot right before the money is needed. People who need to sell their investments within a few years would probably do better in a target-date fund. This is because, as time goes on, the target portfolio gets more conservatively managed, lowering the chances of a big loss.

Index funds may be good for people who won't need to take money out for at least 15 or 20 years. For example, a woman in her 40s who is saving for retirement might do well to buy an index fund and keep it until she is 65 or 70 since the index has had average annual returns of 8% to 10% over that time. Even if the market drops right before she retires, she may still do better than a target-date fund because she earned more over a longer period.

Dollar Cost Averaging vs. Lump Sum Investing

When it comes to investing in the stock market, the main difference between dollar-cost averaging and lump-sum investing lies in the flexibility of where you put your money. Dollar-cost averaging empowers you to regularly invest small amounts over time, adapting to your financial situation. In contrast, lump-sum investing requires you to invest all of your money at once, which may not be as flexible.

Averaging Dollar Costs

Dollar-cost averaging, a strategy that can yield significant long-term benefits, involves regularly investing your money into stocks and ETFs, such as once a week, once a month, or once every three months (often referred to as DCA). This approach, similar to our 401(k) contributions at work, allows us to consistently invest, regardless of market conditions. Over time, this can lead to substantial growth in our investments, potentially multiplying our initial investment. This is the power of dollar-cost averaging, which ensures that you're not overly exposed to market volatility and can benefit from the potential growth of your investments over time.

If you want to use dollar-cost averaging, there is another way to do it besides this one. You can choose to invest a large amount of money over some time. For example, if you have a lot of money in a savings account, you can do this. If you have $20,000 saved up, you might invest it in different ways over a year instead of all at once.

This method is highly recommended because it keeps you from putting all of your money into the stock market at once, which could cause the market to crash and your portfolio's value to drop. Dollar-cost averaging lets you put your money in riskier assets (like stocks) without "feeling" the risk as much. This is because past performance is just a piece of data, and no one can predict what will happen in the future.

Investing All at Once

On the other hand, lump-sum investing means putting all of your money into the stock market at once. If you want to invest right away, you don't have to wait like with dollar-cost averaging; it all goes straight into your chosen assets. Right now, the line between DCA and lump-sum investment is very thin. Let me explain. Lump-sum investing offers the advantage of immediate investment, allowing you to take advantage of potential market gains without delay.

Another name for this is dollar-cost averaging. This is when you save money to invest later. You can still invest every month, though, and think of it as one big investment. Let's say you get a $10,000 bonus every three months. Every time you get a bonus, you choose to put it to work. This is still lump-sum investing, even if you pay for it over time. This is because you're not putting money away for a bad day.

Instead, you could divide the $10,000 bonus into three equal monthly payments over the next three months. This is called dollar-cost averaging. It might seem like a small difference, but if you look at the numbers, it could mean that you have more or less money in your portfolio (more on this below).

Who should use dollar-cost averaging, and who shouldn't?

Dollar-cost averaging is great for investors who are nervous, don't want to take risks and have a lot of money in a high-yield savings account. One way to lower your risk is to break up your investment into smaller pieces and keep the money in a safer place, like a CD.

Dollar-cost averaging can also help you make money if you can spread out your investment over a longer period. If you invest your money too quickly (for example, in three to six months), the market might not have time to get back to normal after a big drop or rise.

Dollar-cost averaging is great for nervous investors who don't want to take risks and have a lot of money in a high-yield savings account. One way to lower your risk is to break up your investment into smaller pieces and keep the money in a safer place, like a CD.

Dollar-cost averaging can also help you make money if you can spread out your investment over a longer time. If you invest your money too quickly (for example, in three to six months), the market might not have time to get back to normal after a big drop or rise.

Who should invest a lump sum, and who shouldn't?

- Invest a lump sum when you are willing to take on a significant amount of risk.
- Consider lump-sum investing if you have a large sum of money to invest, such as $20,000.

- Be prepared for potential market fluctuations, as seen during events like the March drop due to the coronavirus pandemic.
- Suitable for individuals who have the financial capacity to invest and are comfortable with the risk of potential losses.
- Those who don't mind the possibility of losing their investment may find lump-sum investing to be a viable option.
- Highlight the potential for substantial gains, such as if one had invested during the market crash in March and benefited from the subsequent rebound.

When you invest a large sum of money, you need to be willing to take on a lot of risk. It's a risk. People who use the lump sum method say that if you have $20,000 to invest, you should put it all in investments at once. You could see the stock market drop soon if you do this (just like what happened in March due to the coronavirus pandemic). That's why it's called a gamble: it could go up and win you money. If you have money to invest and don't mind losing it, then lump-sum investing is an excellent option for you. Even though there is a risk, there is also the chance of huge rewards. Think about what would have happened if you had put $20,000 into the stock market right after it crashed in March. So far, you'd have been able to ride the wave of a big market bounce.

The same goes for people who are worried about losing their investment or who would instead save some extra money for emergencies than invest it. Lump-sum investing is probably not for these people. Some people are emotionally uncomfortable with the investment, even if they can convince themselves to make it. These people would then trade based on their feelings, which is never a good thing.

What should You Choose?

Yes and no at the same time. In terms of people and psychology, no, it doesn't matter. But in terms of data and statistics, YES, it does. What I mean is that I like to think of this argument as being like

Dave Ramsey's "Debt Snowball" argument. From a mathematical point of view, the Debt Snowball doesn't make sense. Ramsey says to pay off the smallest amount first, then the next biggest, and so on. This method doesn't take interest rates into account, so it's not the most logical, but it works for some people.

That's where I think dollar-cost averaging does better than investing all at once. It doesn't always make sense mathematically, and I'll explain why in a moment, but it gives you peace of mind about your investment plan by letting you keep cash on hand in case of an emergency while also investing some money.

What the polls show

Dollar-cost averaging has problems, just like any other way to lower your risk when investing, like buying bonds. To put it simply, an investor who uses dollar-cost averaging will miss out on big market changes because they are saving money for the next regular deposit toward that investment. By the time the money is ready to be invested, the market may have already turned around, and you will have missed the gain.

Two finance professors did research in the early 1990s that looked at stock market data from the past that went back about 70 years. The results of their study showed that, on average, people who invest all at once get better returns in the first year than people who use dollar-cost averaging and slowly add to their accounts each month.

A new study from Vanguard looked at the difference between investing a lump sum and using dollar-cost averaging in a 60/40 (stocks and bonds) portfolio in three different countries. They found that in every market, investing a lump sum led to higher portfolio values about two-thirds of the time. They did different versions of this test and got results that were mostly the same.

How to invest: step-by-step

Buying stock in a publicly traded company is what it means to invest in stocks. Buying these small pieces is called investing in the company's stock, and it means you think the business will do well and grow over time. If this happens, your shares might become more valuable, and other investors might be willing to pay more than you paid for them. That means you might make money if you decide to sell them.

1. Make a decision on how you wish to invest in the stock market.

There are different ways to invest in stocks. Pick the method that best fits how you want to invest and how involved you want to be in picking the shares you want to buy.

A. "I'd want to select my own stocks and mutual funds." Continue reading; this essay deconstructs what novice investors need to know, such as how to select the best account for your requirements and how to compare stock investments.

B. "I'd prefer a professional to oversee the procedure for me." You could be a good fit for a Robo-advisor, which is a business that provides low-cost financial management. Almost all of the major brokerage firms, as well as many independent advisers, provide these services, which invest your money for you depending on your individual objectives.

C. I'd want to participate in my company's 401(k) plan. This is a common entry point for novice investors. It teaches rookie investors some of the most tried-and-true investing practices, such as making little monthly payments, focusing on the long term, and taking a hands-off approach. Stock mutual funds, but not individual stocks, are often available for investment in 401(k) plans.

2. Choose an investing account

Most of the time, you need a brokerage account to invest in stocks. Making a brokerage account is often part of this for people who like to work with their hands.

Opening a brokerage account

Most likely, the fastest and least expensive way to buy stocks, funds, and other things is through an online brokerage account. An individual retirement account, or IRA, can be opened with a broker. If you're already saving for retirement through a 401(k) or another plan through your job, you can also open a taxable brokerage account.

3. Discover the distinction between investing in stocks and investing in funds.

Doing things on your own? Don't stress out. Putting money into stocks doesn't have to be hard. For most people, investing in the stock market means choosing between two types of investments:

Stock mutual funds or exchange-traded funds. In a mutual fund transaction, you can buy small amounts of several stocks at once. ETFs and index funds are both types of mutual funds that follow an index. For example, a Standard & Poor's 500 fund buys shares in the companies that make up the index to copy it. If you put money into a fund, you get a small share of each of these companies. You can make a diverse portfolio by combining different funds. It's important to note that equity mutual funds are another name for stock mutual funds.

Individual stocks. Spreading out your investments across many shares is possible, but it takes work and research. Keep in mind that individual stocks will go up and down if you choose this route. If you look into a company and decide to invest in it, calm down and think about why you chose that company in the first place.

One good thing about stock mutual funds is that they are already diversified, which lowers your risk. The most obvious choice for most investors, especially those who are saving for retirement, is a portfolio made up mostly of mutual funds.

However, mutual funds are not likely to rise as quickly as some individual stocks. If you buy individual stocks wisely, they can pay off handsomely, but the chances of any one stock making you rich are pretty low.

4. Make a plan for your stock market investment.

At this point in the process, new investors usually have two questions:

I want to buy stocks. How much money do I need? An exchange-traded fund (ETF) might be the best choice for you if you want mutual funds but don't have a lot of money. Mutual funds sometimes have minimums of $1,000 or more. ETFs, on the other hand, trade like stocks, so you pay a share price (which can be less than $100).

How much cash should I put into stocks? Haven't we already said that most financial advisors recommend investing in funds? If you plan to keep your investments for a long time, you might put a big chunk of your money into stock funds. A 30-year-old person who is saving for retirement might have 80% of their money in stock funds and 20% in bond funds. But individual stocks are a whole different story. Usually, you should only put them in a small part of your investment portfolio.

5. Focus on investing for the long-term

Putting money into stocks has been shown to be a very good way to get rich over time. The stock market has had an average annual return of about 10% for many decades. But remember that this is just an average for the market as a whole. Some years will be better than others, and the returns on different stocks may be different as well. For long-term investors, the stock market is a great place to put their money no matter what happens today or next year; what they're looking for is the long-term average.

There are a lot of different strategies and approaches you can use when trading, but some of the smartest investors have stuck to the basics of the stock market. That usually means putting most of your money into funds—Warren Buffett famously said that a low-cost S&P 500 index fund is the best investment most Americans can make—and only buying individual stocks if you think the company will do well in the long term.

It is very hard not to look at your stocks or mutual funds when you first start investing in them. It's not a good idea to check your stocks several times a day, every day, unless you want to beat the odds and become a great day trader.

6. Take care of your stock portfolio

It's not good for your portfolio or your mental health to check on your stocks every day, but there are times when you need to. If you want to use the above methods to build a portfolio of stocks and mutual funds over time, you should check in with it once a year to make sure it's still helping you reach your goals.

Here are some things to think about. People often move some of their stocks into safer fixed-income investments as they get closer to retirement. If most of your money is in one industry, you might want to buy stocks or funds from a different one to spread out your risk. Finally, you might want to think about expanding your business to other areas. Vanguard says that you should put up to 40% of your portfolio in foreign stocks for the best results. You might be able to get this chance through mutual funds that buy stocks in other countries.

Layers of Investing
An Investment Pyramid

Investment pyramids, which are also called risk pyramids, are a way to divide up assets based on risk. This method figures out how risky an investment is by looking at how much the return on the investment changes or how likely it is that the investment will lose a lot of value. If you look at the pyramid, the bottom and widest parts are low-risk investments, the middle part is growth investments, and the top part is speculative investments.

Understanding the Investment Pyramid

With the lowest-risk assets at the bottom of an investing pyramid, established company equity securities are put in the middle, and speculative securities are put at the top.

- The broadest part of the pyramid, called the base, would have the most assets. It would be made up of cash, CDs, short-term government bonds, and money market instruments.

- In the middle of the pyramid, there should be a fair amount of corporate bonds, stocks, and real estate. There is a small chance that these investments will lose value, but they are expected to earn money over time.

- The very top would have the smallest allocation weights and would contain very risky, speculative assets that have a high chance of losing money but also a chance of making more than average profits. Some of these are derivative contracts like options and futures (which aren't used for hedging), alternative investments, and collectibles like art.

As you move up the pyramid, the level of risk takes a bigger bite out of the total assets that can be invested. Because of this, as you move up the pyramid, the risk goes up but so does the reward.

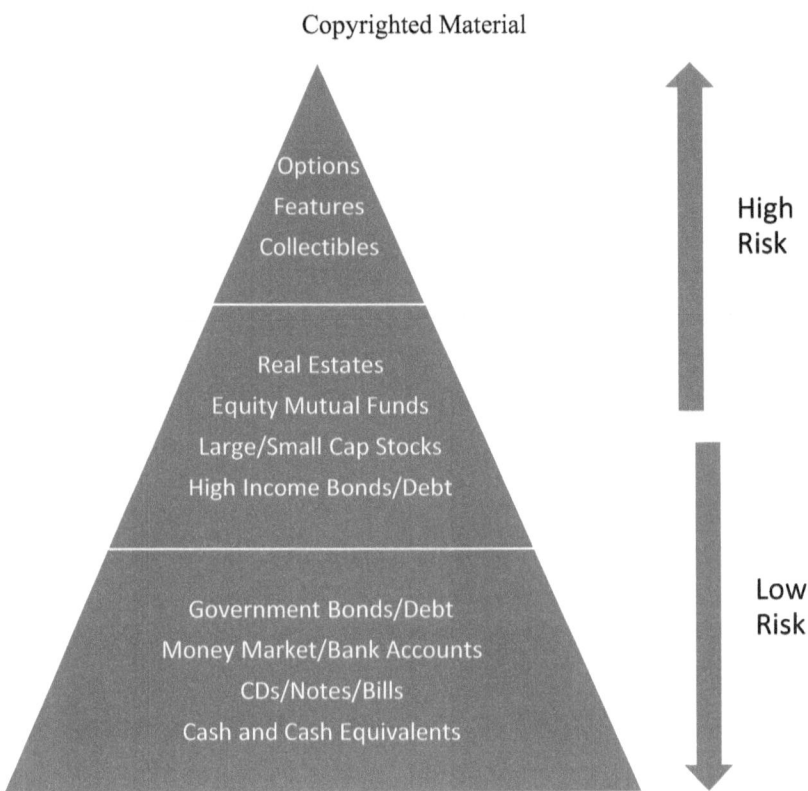

www.ingramcontent.com/pod-product-compliance
Lightning Source LLC
Chambersburg PA
CBHW031433210526
45464CB00005B/2182